4 GENERATIONS

1 WORKFORCE

0 HAPPY EMPLOYEES

BY

ADAM J. SAN JUAN

Copyright © 2025 by Adam J. San Juan

All rights reserved.

No part of this book may be reproduced, stored in a retrieval system, or transmitted in any form or by any means—electronic, mechanical, photocopying, recording, or otherwise—without prior written permission from the author or publisher, except as permitted by U.S. copyright law.

Disclaimer

This publication is intended to provide accurate and authoritative information on the subject matter covered. It is sold with the understanding that the author and publisher are not engaged in rendering legal, investment, accounting, or other professional services. While every effort has been made to ensure the accuracy and completeness of the information, the author and publisher make no warranties, express or implied, regarding its content, including, without limitation, warranties of merchantability or fitness for a particular purpose.

The strategies and advice presented herein may not be suitable for all readers or circumstances. Readers are encouraged to seek professional guidance tailored to their specific needs. Neither the author nor the publisher shall be held liable for any damages, including but not limited to, special, incidental, consequential, or other damages arising directly or indirectly from the use of the information contained in this book.

Regulatory Disclosure

Adam J. San Juan is a financial advisor licensed with FINRA. In compliance with industry regulations, Argo Publishing is listed as an Outside Business Activity (OBA) with the author's broker-dealer. This book is an independent work of the author and is not sponsored, endorsed, or reviewed by any financial regulatory agency. The opinions expressed in this book are solely those of the author and do not necessarily reflect the views of any financial institution, regulatory body, or employer. This book does not offer financial, investment, or legal advice.

Publishing Information

Published by: Argo Publishing
Berwyn, IL

Printed in the United States of America

First Edition: 2025

For those who shaped, stretched, and strengthened me, proving that people are the path to prosperity.

"The old believe everything, the middle-aged suspect everything, the young know everything."

— Oscar Wilde

Table of Contents

ON PURPOSE 11
   WHAT QUALIFIES ME TO WRITE THIS? 11
   WHY WAS THIS BOOK WRITTEN? 13
   WHO IS THIS BOOK FOR? 15

WELL, WTF IS HAPPENING IN THE WORKFORCE? 17
   WHY GENERATIONAL DIFFERENCES MATTER IN BUSINESS 19
   MYTHS VS. REALITIES OF GENERATIONAL WORK HABITS 21
   HOW HIRING, RETENTION, AND MOTIVATION HAVE EVOLVED 23

CHAPTER 1: SILENT GENERATION – THE LEGACY LEADERS 25
   OVERVIEW OF THEIR WORK ETHIC AND LEADERSHIP STYLE 29
   WHY THEY'RE STILL VALUABLE IN CONSULTING, MENTORSHIP, AND BOARD ROLES 36
   PRACTICAL TOOLS: BEST WAYS TO LEVERAGE THEIR EXPERIENCE BEFORE RETIREMENT 44

CHAPTER 2: BABY BOOMERS – THE WORKAHOLICS TURNED MENTORS 52
   THEIR IMPACT ON CORPORATE CULTURE AND LEADERSHIP 57
   STRUGGLES WITH REMOTE WORK, DIGITAL TRANSFORMATION, AND YOUNGER LEADERSHIP 63
   PRACTICAL TOOLS: HOW TO RETAIN THEIR KNOWLEDGE WHILE INTEGRATING MODERN WORKPLACE PRACTICES 70

CHAPTER 3: GEN X – THE NO-BS MANAGERS 78
   THE INDEPENDENT PROBLEM-SOLVERS WHO DISLIKE MICROMANAGEMENT 83
   HOW THEY BRIDGE THE GAP BETWEEN BOOMERS AND MILLENNIALS 91
   PRACTICAL TOOLS: EFFECTIVE LEADERSHIP STRATEGIES AND ENGAGEMENT TECHNIQUES FOR GEN X 98

CHAPTER 4: MILLENNIALS – THE PURPOSE-DRIVEN EMPLOYEES 105
   WORK-LIFE BALANCE, MISSION-DRIVEN WORK, AND JOB-HOPPING TENDENCIES 109
   HOW TO KEEP MILLENNIALS ENGAGED WITHOUT BURNOUT 115

PRACTICAL TOOLS: BEST WAYS TO RETAIN AND DEVELOP MILLENNIALS IN LEADERSHIP ROLES 122

CHAPTER 5: GEN Z – THE DIGITAL DISRUPTORS 130

DIGITAL NATIVES WHO WHO EXPECT MORE THAN JUST TECHNOLOGY 134
WHY THEIR COMMUNICATION STYLE AND WORK EXPECTATIONS CAN FRUSTRATE OLDER WORKERS 141
PRACTICAL TOOLS: HOW TO ATTRACT, MOTIVATE, AND RETAIN GEN Z EMPLOYEES 148

CHAPTER 6: GEN ALPHA – THE FUTURE OF WORK 156

PREDICTIONS ON HOW GEN ALPHA WILL SHAPE THE WORKFORCE 160
HOW AI, AUTOMATION, AND NEW LEARNING METHODS WILL REDEFINE EMPLOYMENT 166
PRACTICAL TOOLS: WHAT BUSINESS OWNERS NEED TO PREPARE FOR NOW 173

CHAPTER 7: MANAGING A MULTIGENERATIONAL WORKFORCE 181

HOW TO PREVENT GENERATIONAL CONFLICTS IN THE WORKPLACE 183
THE BEST LEADERSHIP AND COMMUNICATION STYLES FOR EACH GROUP 191
PRACTICAL TOOLS: GENERATIONAL COMMUNICATION CHEAT SHEET AND TEAM-BUILDING STRATEGIES 199

CHAPTER 8: WTF HAPPENS NEXT? 206

THE FUTURE OF HIRING, RETENTION, AND COMPANY CULTURE 208
THE BIGGEST GENERATIONAL SHIFTS COMING IN THE NEXT DECADE 215
PRACTICAL TOOLS: SELF-ASSESSMENT FOR BUSINESS OWNERS TO MEASURE THEIR GENERATIONAL AWARENESS 222

I CALL "BS" 231

SO, THE FUTURE OF WORK IS NOW 237

AFTERWORD 242

ACKNOWLEDGEMENTS 244

ADDITIONAL RESOURCES 246

ABOUT THE AUTHOR 249

Foreword

It was Filipino Restaurant Week in the Chicagoland area. As part of a Chicago Chapter Non-Profit Organization, we spent countless weeks preparing for this event. Reaching out to small businesses, brainstorming incentives, and trying to find ways to capture the attention of whole communities: the young hip kids, the loyal regulars, and those looking to be a part of something greater than just another meal. Enter Adam San Juan...the someone looking to be a part of something greater.

Adam reached out to us this week in order to gain a better understanding of our efforts and organization. Needless to say, a few phone calls, a couple lunches, and a round of golf later, I had bought into his natural leadership and mentorship. I admire his curiosity and genuine interest in nurturing relationships with people, his desire to understand all walks of people without judgement, and his open-mindedness.

Gen WTF, Adam's new project addressing generational differences in the workplace. A hot button topic that all workplaces are seeking answers to. Adam is the guy to envelop a universal audience of professionals through a functional guidebook of how to be more successful as a business in this area. He eloquently addresses the "WHYs" that employers are struggling with: Why do we need each generation in the room? Why do we have to understand how each generation operates to grow? Why is it important as an employer to have a basic appreciation for who you are hiring?

I come from a workplace with a healthy representation of the four generations highlighted in this book. A millennial myself (a generation driven by purpose) and in a position of leadership, I continually challenge myself each day to find ways to connect with each generation on a playing field that feels understood and respected by everyone. *Gen WTF* provides tools to help bridge this gap more effectively, but most importantly, it provides perspective on why "we are who we are" and our importance, in respect to our generation. Adam provides the reader with a launchpad to start your journey of understanding in hopes you will continue to explore beyond the pages.

Whether you are a leader or business owner, the need to adapt and understand your employees is vital to achieving overall success. In order to leverage their strengths, you have to acknowledge their roots. In order to grow, you have to strategize and compromise. While this will not change overnight, with open-mindedness and practice, your outlook on your leadership approach with the generations will flourish. Adam San Juan and *Gen WTF*, undoubtedly, provide the tools for this navigation. Bridge the Gaps. Foster Respect. Find Success.

Andrew Guerrero, CPA
Chicago, Illinois

Author's Note on Objectivity

This book was written without political affiliation, agenda, or allegiance. The purpose of *Gen WTF* is not to take sides—but to provide clarity, context, and tools for navigating the complex reality of today's workforce.

You'll see terms like flexibility, purpose, fairness, inclusion, and even DEI—not because they belong to one political party or movement, but because they reflect real values that today's employees care about. These concepts have been politicized in public discourse, but their underlying intentions—to recognize people, create belonging, and improve access to opportunity—are fundamentally human.

This book seeks to honor the spirit of those intentions, especially in environments where generational differences already present enough challenges. If the language in these pages makes you pause or feel uncomfortable, I invite you not to disengage—but to lean in. The most effective leaders I know aren't the ones who agree with every trend or buzzword; they're the ones who ask, "What does this mean for my people?"

At its core, *Gen WTF* is not about being politically correct—it's about being people-correct. Because when you lead with curiosity, empathy, and a commitment to understanding, you build better teams. And that's something every generation deserves.

On Purpose

Every book has a purpose, a reason it exists beyond just words on a page. *Gen WTF* was written to solve a very real problem: generational misunderstandings in the workplace are costing businesses time, money, and relationships. But this book isn't just about diagnosing the problem—it's about offering practical, actionable solutions in a way that simplifies the complexity of multigenerational dynamics.

What Qualifies Me to Write This?

For over 30 years, I've dedicated myself to understanding human behavior—why people think the way they do, how they make decisions, and how those decisions impact their lives and businesses. My work has always focused on helping people see the world more clearly and navigate human interactions more effectively.

I've written two books that tackle the fundamental conflicts humans face:

- *What Are You Looking At? The Impact of Answering and How It Changes Everything* (2023)—Focused on human interactions, communication, and the power of perception (Man vs. Man).

- *What Am I Doing Here? A Guide to the Unseen Influence of Your Surroundings* (2024)—Focused on how environments shape decisions and experiences (Man vs. Environment).
- My third book, *What Was I Thinking?* (TBD, late 2025/early 2026), will explore decision-making and internal conflict (Man vs. Himself).

These books form what I call the "*Human Series*", designed to help people better understand themselves and those around them. I've had the privilege of sharing these insights through college presentations, corporate workshops, and podcast interviews, where I've spoken on how people interact, communicate, and navigate conflict.

So why write *Gen WTF*? Because generational conflict is one of the most overlooked barriers to success in today's workplace. Through my work with business owners, managers, and sales professionals, I've seen firsthand how misunderstandings between generations lead to hiring struggles, retention issues, employee disengagement, and leadership challenges. And too often, instead of taking the time to understand their workforce, leaders throw up their hands and say, "It is what it is."

I wrote this book because it doesn't have to be that way.

Why Was This Book Written?

The human side of running a business is often the hardest part. Business owners master their craft, their numbers, and their strategies—but when it comes to leading people, many struggle. And a big part of that struggle comes from not understanding how different generations approach work, leadership, and engagement.

Over the years, I've seen the same problems play out repeatedly:

- Hiring frustrations—Business owners can't find the "right" people because they don't understand how different generations evaluate job opportunities.
- Retention struggles—Employees leave because their needs and values aren't recognized.
- Workplace tension—Leaders expect younger employees to operate like older ones, and vice versa.
- Productivity issues—Communication gaps and outdated management styles kill efficiency.
- Client relationships suffer—Because people sell and buy differently across generations.

I wrote this book because I've watched good business owners lose great employees simply because they didn't take the time to understand what motivated them. I've seen companies waste money on one-size-fits-all hiring strategies that don't work across generations. I've seen sales teams struggle because they don't realize their approach lands differently depending on who they're selling to.

And most of all, I've seen leaders make unnecessary mistakes—not because they're bad at business, but because no one ever gave them a simple, actionable way to bridge generational gaps.

That's what *Gen WTF* is: a shortcut to understanding and solving these problems.

This book isn't about making leaders experts in generational theory. It's about giving them tools they can use right away to:

- Hire better.
- Retain key employees.
- Lead more effectively.
- Build stronger relationships with both employees and clients.
- Make their workplace more productive and engaging.

And it doesn't require implementing everything in the book—just one or two small changes can make a major impact.

Who Is This Book For?

This book is for anyone who interacts with people. While it's written with business owners, managers, and HR professionals in mind, its insights are relevant for salespeople, team leaders, employees, and even job seekers. Whether you're hiring, leading, selling, or just trying to understand your coworkers, this book will help you navigate generational differences with more clarity and confidence.

- Business Owners & Managers—If you've struggled with hiring, retention, or workplace engagement, this book will help you understand what's driving those challenges and how to fix them.
- HR & Recruiting Professionals—Learn how to tailor job descriptions, interview strategies, and benefits packages to attract and retain top talent across generations.
- Sales & Client-Facing Roles—Understanding how different generations make buying decisions can transform how you sell and communicate with clients.
- Employees & Job Seekers—If you've ever felt misunderstood at work or want to know how to position yourself effectively across generations, this book will give you insights into how leadership thinks.
- Anyone in Leadership or Team Collaboration—Generational dynamics affect how teams work together, how ideas are received, and how workplace culture develops. This book will

help you be a better communicator, problem solver, and leader—no matter your role.

While this book is designed for those actively facing workplace challenges, it's just as valuable for those preparing for them. If you're about to hire, step into leadership, or enter a new workplace, the insights here can give you an edge before problems arise.

At its core, *Gen WTF* is about helping people see beyond generational stereotypes and focus on what really matters—building workplaces that work for everyone. And when we do that, everyone wins.

—

Generational differences aren't the problem—our lack of understanding about them is. This book exists to change that. The goal isn't to convince you that one generation is better than another. It's to give you the tools to navigate the differences effectively.

By the end of this book, my hope is that you'll see your workforce differently, communicate more effectively, and make small adjustments that lead to big results. You don't need to overhaul your entire approach—just take a few insights, apply them, and see what happens.

This book is a roadmap. Where you go with it is up to you.

Well, WTF Is Happening in the Workforce?

The job posting went up at 8 AM. By noon, the hiring manager had received 200 applications. The CEO—a Baby Boomer—wanted a candidate with a 'strong work ethic, proven loyalty, and a willingness to put in the hours.' The hiring manager—a Millennial—was looking for "a culture fit, someone who values flexibility and innovation." By 5 PM, an argument broke out: Why was no one on the same page about what "a good employee" looks like?

The modern workforce is a melting pot of generations, each shaped by distinct historical events, technological advancements, and social movements. Business owners today face the challenge of managing employees with wildly different expectations, communication styles, and work ethics. Understanding these generational nuances isn't just a trendy HR topic—it's a critical business strategy for hiring, retention, and productivity.

With Baby Boomers delaying retirement, Millennials stepping into leadership, and Gen Z entering the workforce, workplaces have never been more generationally diverse. The traditional model of a senior workforce mentoring younger employees has evolved into something far more complex: seasoned professionals learning new technology from younger colleagues, Millennials pushing for work-life balance, and Gen Z demanding transparency, flexibility, and purpose-driven work.

The challenge? These differences can either drive collaboration or create conflict—depending on how well business owners and managers adapt. A Boomer leader who expects loyalty and structured work may feel frustrated by a Millennial's preference for remote work and job-hopping. A Gen X manager who values autonomy might struggle to understand why Gen Z employees crave constant feedback and engagement. And while younger employees may see themselves as pushing progress forward, older employees may view those same behaviors as entitlement or impatience.

To build an effective, engaged workforce, leaders must recognize that generational diversity is an asset, not a liability. Employees of all ages bring valuable perspectives, skills, and problem-solving approaches—if companies learn to harness them correctly.

Why Generational Differences Matter in Business

Generational dynamics influence everything from workplace culture to innovation, collaboration, and company performance. A Boomer manager may value in-person meetings and hierarchical decision-making, while a Gen Z employee prefers digital communication and flatter leadership structures. If business owners fail to recognize these differences, they risk disengagement, high turnover, and workplace friction.

These generational differences don't just affect internal operations—they directly impact customer engagement as well. A company that markets to Millennials on Instagram must also maintain a strong phone-based customer service model for Boomers. A brand that embraces TikTok trends for Gen Z needs to ensure they aren't alienating Gen X customers who may find that approach off-putting.

Here's why businesses can't afford to ignore generational shifts:
- Hiring & Retention Depend on It: Each generation has different motivators when choosing and staying at a job. Millennials prioritize work-life balance and professional growth, while Boomers may value stability and pension plans. Understanding these priorities helps companies attract and retain talent more effectively.
- Leadership Needs to Evolve: One-size-fits-all leadership no longer works. A top-down, authoritarian approach might have

been effective in the past, but younger generations respond better to collaborative leadership and transparency.
- Innovation Requires Cross-Generational Input: When companies successfully blend experience with fresh ideas, they foster creativity and innovation. Gen Z's digital fluency paired with Baby Boomers' industry expertise can lead to groundbreaking solutions—if companies create environments where these ideas can coexist.

The companies that adapt to generational expectations will build strong, resilient workforces. The ones that resist? They'll struggle with employee dissatisfaction, retention issues, and cultural disconnects.

Myths vs. Realities of Generational Work Habits

Generational stereotypes run rampant in the workplace, leading to misunderstandings that can create unnecessary conflict. Let's break down some of the biggest myths and the realities behind them.

Myth 1: Millennials Are Entitled and Unwilling to Work Hard

Reality: Millennials aren't lazy—they just reject outdated work norms. They were raised in an era where career stability was shattered by economic downturns, student loan debt, and automation replacing traditional jobs. This generation prioritizes work-life balance, professional development, and purpose-driven careers—not because they're entitled, but because they've seen what happens when companies don't invest in employee well-being.

Myth 2: Baby Boomers Refuse to Embrace Technology

Reality: While Boomers didn't grow up with smartphones, they've adapted to digital tools out of necessity and practicality. In fact, many Boomers embraced tech before younger generations were even born—they were the pioneers of the personal computer revolution, after all. Their hesitancy toward certain modern tools isn't about resistance; it's about needing time to learn and adapt.

Myth 3: Gen X Is Disengaged and Cynical About Work

Reality: Gen X is one of the most adaptable and resilient generations. They grew up as latchkey kids, learned to be independent early, and prefer autonomy in the workplace. If they seem disengaged, it's often because they don't demand constant attention like Millennials and Gen Z. They value results over busywork and expect to be judged by their contributions, not their presence in a cubicle from 9 to 5.

Myth 4: Gen Z Lacks Attention Spans and Loyalty

Reality: Gen Z processes information faster than any previous generation—not because they can't focus, but because they've grown up in an era of digital overload. Their ability to multitask, scan data quickly, and adapt to changing information makes them exceptional problem-solvers. As for loyalty? Gen Z isn't disloyal—they simply won't tolerate workplaces that lack transparency, purpose, or respect for work-life integration.

While generational traits are influenced by upbringing, culture, and technology, the best workplaces recognize and adapt to employees' unique skills and motivations rather than boxing them into outdated labels.

How Hiring, Retention, and Motivation Have Evolved

Hiring Trends: Then vs. Now
- Then: Employers held the power, and workers competed for limited jobs. Resumes were printed, interviews were in person, and networking happened at business lunches.
- Now: Employees hold more leverage, choosing workplaces based on flexibility, benefits, and culture. Hiring happens through LinkedIn, remote interviews, and AI-driven recruiting platforms.

Retention Challenges: The Shift in Workplace Loyalty
- Then: Loyalty was expected. Employees often stayed with the same company for decades, climbing the corporate ladder.
- Now: Loyalty is earned. Employees, especially Millennials and Gen Z, won't hesitate to leave a company that fails to provide career development, purpose, or work-life balance.

Motivation Factors: What Drives Employees Today?
- Then: Paychecks and promotions were the primary motivators. A steady salary, pension, and title progression were enough to keep employees engaged.
- Now: Purpose and culture matter just as much as money. Employees seek work that aligns with their values, offers flexibility, and provides ongoing skill development.

Generational differences aren't just an HR issue—they impact every facet of business, from hiring and retention to productivity and customer engagement. Companies that embrace generational diversity will build stronger teams, foster innovation, and create workplaces where employees of all ages thrive. But to truly understand where today's workforce is headed, we first need to understand where it's been.

As we dive into the specific characteristics of each generation in the following chapters, remember: the goal isn't to label, but to understand. The modern workplace wasn't built overnight—it was shaped by decades of evolving priorities, leadership styles, and work ethics. And at the foundation of it all is the Silent Generation, whose influence still echoes in boardrooms, policies, and workplace traditions today. By recognizing what drives different generations, business owners can move beyond stereotypes and create a work environment where every employee—regardless of age—feels valued and empowered to contribute.

Chapter 1: Silent Generation – The Legacy Leaders

"The reward for work well done is the opportunity to do more."

— Jonas Salk

Q: *"What does success look like to you?"*

A: *"Success is about stability, hard work, and leaving something meaningful behind. I grew up in a time when jobs were scarce, so just having steady employment was an accomplishment. Success isn't about chasing happiness—it's about fulfilling your responsibilities, providing for your family, and earning the respect of your peers. If you can retire comfortably and know you did your part, that's success."*

The Silent Generation, born between 1928 and 1945, represents a workforce shaped by hardship, resilience, and an unwavering commitment to duty. They grew up during the Great Depression and World War II, experiencing economic scarcity and global uncertainty, which instilled in them an enduring work ethic, deep loyalty, and a respect for authority. These experiences made them disciplined, pragmatic, and often self-sacrificing when it comes to their careers and responsibilities. Unlike later generations who prioritize work-life balance, the Silent Generation viewed work as both a privilege and a necessity—something to be done without complaint, with a steadfast commitment to excellence.

Although their numbers in the workforce have dwindled as many have entered retirement, their influence continues to be felt across industries. In corporate boardrooms, consulting roles, and advisory positions, the Silent Generation continues to serve as an essential bridge between traditional business values and the evolving expectations of younger professionals. They offer something that cannot be replicated by younger generations: decades of hard-earned wisdom, a deep institutional memory, and a leadership style rooted in long-term stability rather than short-term gains.

Despite the perception that they are simply phasing out of the workforce, many members of this generation remain active in business. Whether by choice or necessity, they continue to contribute in ways that modern companies often undervalue. In an era driven by speed and disruption, they offer stability and patience. In a time where digital communication dominates, they bring a preference for face-to-face interaction and relationship-building. And while today's workforce leans toward job-hopping and rapid career pivots, they emphasize loyalty, commitment, and legacy-building.

Yet, their role is shifting. The Silent Generation is no longer the dominant leadership force, but they remain critical players in mentorship, strategic decision-making, and maintaining cultural continuity within organizations. Business owners and executives who understand their value can leverage their experience to strengthen their companies rather than allowing their expertise to fade into irrelevance.

The next sections of this chapter will explore what makes the Silent Generation unique in terms of leadership and work ethic, why their experience remains invaluable in advisory and mentorship roles, and how business owners can effectively utilize their strengths before they step away from the workforce entirely. By the time you finish this chapter, you'll have a clearer understanding of why this generation still matters—and how you can ensure their wisdom isn't lost as they transition into retirement.

Overview of Their Work Ethic and Leadership Style

The Silent Generation's work ethic is deeply rooted in the values of perseverance, responsibility, and unwavering dedication to their careers. Unlike younger generations who prioritize work-life balance and professional fulfillment, this generation was raised with the mindset that hard work is not only expected but also a defining characteristic of personal success. For many in this generation, work was not simply a means to an end—it was a lifelong commitment, a duty that was meant to be honored with discipline and sacrifice.

The Foundations of Their Work Ethic

Members of the Silent Generation were shaped by economic instability and global uncertainty. Many grew up in households where financial security was fragile, and survival often depended on relentless perseverance. These early experiences instilled in them a deep respect for employment, viewing jobs as opportunities that should not be taken for granted. As a result, the Silent Generation developed a reputation for being highly reliable, hardworking, and fiercely dedicated employees.

Unlike modern professionals who seek rapid career progression and personal fulfillment, Silent Generation workers were more likely to remain with a single employer for decades. They valued stability over change and saw longevity in a company as a mark of personal and professional achievement. This sense of loyalty was often reciprocated by employers, who rewarded long-term employees with pensions, job security, and incremental promotions—practices that have become far less common in today's workforce.

Another key characteristic of their work ethic is an aversion to unnecessary risk. Having lived through economic downturns, wars, and financial instability, they tend to make conservative financial and career decisions. Many preferred working in industries that provided stable, predictable career paths, such as manufacturing, government roles, or corporate management. They were also more likely to adhere to structured career trajectories, believing that success was a gradual process earned through experience and dedication rather than rapid advancement or job-hopping.

The Silent Generation also placed a strong emphasis on professionalism, believing that work should be conducted with formality and respect. Unlike today's more casual work environments, they were accustomed to dress codes, structured business etiquette, and clear lines of authority. Professionalism was not only a workplace expectation but also a reflection of personal integrity and discipline.

Leadership Style: Stability, Authority, and Responsibility

As leaders, members of the Silent Generation tend to embrace traditional hierarchical structures, where authority is respected, and decisions are made by those with the most experience. They value order, consistency, and long-term planning, prioritizing steady growth over rapid, high-risk expansion. Unlike younger generations who often favor participative leadership, the Silent Generation's approach is top-down, structured, and directive.

One of their greatest strengths as leaders is their ability to provide stability in times of uncertainty. Because they lived through economic recessions, wartime rationing, and fluctuating job markets, they developed a pragmatic approach to leadership that focuses on resilience and calculated decision-making. They are not impulsive; they rely on proven methods and past experiences to guide their choices.

They also emphasize accountability and discipline within their leadership. Employees were expected to demonstrate commitment, follow company policies, and respect the chain of command. Unlike modern approaches that encourage informal collaboration between different levels of an organization, the Silent Generation's leadership style was often built on a more formal and structured dynamic. Titles, roles, and reporting structures carried significant weight in their professional world.

Additionally, their leadership style often involved a strong focus on long-term success rather than short-term gains. They were less likely to chase trends or disrupt business models hastily; instead, they preferred steady, measured growth that ensured the sustainability of a company or institution. This approach, while sometimes viewed as resistant to change, has allowed many organizations to build legacies of stability that have lasted for decades.

Challenges in Today's Workforce

While their leadership strengths have been invaluable for decades, the Silent Generation's approach can sometimes clash with today's evolving workforce expectations. Younger employees, particularly Millennials and Gen Z, seek collaborative leadership, transparency, and flexibility—qualities that may not always align with the structured, authoritative style favored by Silent Generation leaders.

Additionally, their preference for in-person meetings, formal business communication, and traditional office culture can sometimes feel out of step with a workforce that increasingly embraces remote work, digital collaboration tools, and casual workplace interactions. However, these differences do not make their leadership style obsolete. Instead, businesses must find ways to integrate their experience and wisdom into modern workplaces while allowing for necessary adaptation.

For example, while Silent Generation leaders may prefer a structured, in-office setting, they can be encouraged to share their institutional knowledge through mentorship programs or advisory roles rather than micromanaging day-to-day operations. Additionally, their experience in crisis management and economic resilience is invaluable in industries that face frequent disruptions. Modern businesses can learn from their ability to remain composed and decisive during volatile periods.

Why Their Work Ethic Still Matters

In a business environment where job-hopping is common and corporate loyalty is diminishing, the Silent Generation's dedication and perseverance serve as important reminders of the value of commitment. While younger generations may focus on rapid career advancement, they can benefit greatly from the Silent Generation's approach to steady, disciplined growth.

Moreover, their emphasis on responsibility and accountability continues to be a vital lesson in leadership. Business owners who recognize the strengths of Silent Generation leaders can use their presence to instill discipline, create structured mentorship programs, and reinforce the importance of institutional knowledge.

Another critical contribution of the Silent Generation is their approach to relationship-building in business. Unlike younger generations who rely heavily on digital networking and quick communication, they cultivated professional relationships through face-to-face interactions, long-term partnerships, and trust-building over time. Their ability to maintain strong business relationships has been a cornerstone of traditional corporate success and remains relevant today, particularly in industries where reputation and client trust are key factors.

Furthermore, as younger generations become increasingly reliant on fast-changing technology and automation, Silent Generation professionals offer the counterbalance of experience, patience, and long-term vision. While innovation is crucial for modern business, stability and measured decision-making remain equally essential. Organizations that recognize the complementary strengths of different generations can create workplaces that balance innovation with wisdom, flexibility with discipline, and rapid growth with sustainability.

As the Silent Generation continues to transition out of the workforce, their legacy remains an integral part of many industries. The values they instilled—hard work, discipline, responsibility, and long-term commitment—are as relevant today as they were decades ago. Businesses that seek to retain their institutional knowledge and leadership wisdom will benefit immensely from finding ways to bridge generational differences while respecting the Silent Generation's time-tested principles.

The next section will explore why their experience remains invaluable in advisory and mentorship roles, highlighting how businesses can best utilize the Silent Generation's wisdom before they retire entirely.

Why They're Still Valuable in Consulting, Mentorship, and Board Roles

The Silent Generation may be stepping away from daily operations in the workforce, but their influence remains invaluable. Even as younger generations take over leadership roles, there is an undeniable benefit to retaining the knowledge and experience of those who came before them. Organizations that recognize the value of the Silent Generation in consulting, mentorship, and board positions are not just preserving history—they're ensuring continuity, stability, and the passing down of generational wisdom.

Consulting: Experience as a Competitive Advantage

With decades of industry expertise, the Silent Generation is uniquely positioned to serve as consultants, providing insights that can only be gained through lived experience. While younger leaders may bring fresh perspectives and innovative ideas, they often lack the historical context and crisis management experience that seasoned professionals bring to the table.

Strategic Guidance for Businesses

Silent Generation consultants help businesses avoid repeating past mistakes by offering long-term, big-picture strategies. Their ability to recall economic cycles, industry shifts, and lessons learned from previous downturns can be invaluable in today's fast-moving markets. They provide historical insights that many younger leaders may not have considered, offering perspective on challenges such as inflation, regulatory changes, and evolving business ethics.

Additionally, Silent Generation consultants are adept at risk management. Having weathered economic recessions, geopolitical conflicts, and financial crises, they provide a steadying presence in industries that require careful long-term planning. Their guidance helps companies avoid reckless decision-making in pursuit of short-term gains.

Crisis Management & Reputation Building

Many businesses find themselves in crisis mode at some point, whether due to economic downturns, public relations scandals, or leadership disruptions. Silent Generation professionals have seen it all before and understand how to navigate challenges with a calm, measured approach. Their ability to provide level-headed advice in high-pressure situations makes them indispensable as consultants during times of uncertainty.

Beyond crisis management, they also offer valuable insights into reputation building. In an age where branding and social perception matter more than ever, the Silent Generation can teach companies how to cultivate trust and credibility over time. While younger businesses may focus on instant visibility and rapid growth, Silent Generation consultants emphasize the importance of integrity, consistency, and long-term relationship building.

Mentorship: Bridging the Generational Gap

While the Silent Generation may not always resonate with the rapid, digital-driven world of younger employees, their mentorship remains one of the most valuable resources for today's workforce. As the workplace grows increasingly diverse in age, the need for cross-generational mentorship has never been greater.

Passing Down Leadership and Soft Skills

Leadership is often learned through observation, and who better to teach it than those who spent decades refining their leadership styles? Silent Generation professionals instill essential soft skills in younger employees, including:

- Discipline and accountability – Ensuring that work is done with integrity and consistency.

- Professionalism and etiquette – Navigating business relationships with respect and diplomacy.
- Patience and resilience – Teaching younger employees how to handle setbacks and long-term career growth.

One of the greatest advantages of mentorship from the Silent Generation is their ability to provide constructive criticism without personal bias. Many younger employees, particularly Millennials and Gen Z, thrive in feedback-rich environments. However, they also struggle with overly critical or impersonal feedback that can feel discouraging. Silent Generation mentors offer feedback from a place of experience rather than competition, helping mentees refine their skills in a nurturing yet professional manner.

Keeping Institutional Knowledge Alive

Every business has its own unique culture, values, and unwritten rules. As longtime employees retire, institutional knowledge is at risk of being lost. Silent Generation mentors help bridge this gap by passing down insights about:

- Company history and evolution – Why certain practices exist and how they developed over time.
- Client and stakeholder relationships – Preserving valuable networks built over decades.

- Industry best practices – Ensuring that hard-earned knowledge is not lost with retirement.

By pairing Silent Generation mentors with younger employees, companies create a legacy of knowledge transfer that ensures stability and consistency even as leadership evolves.

Board Roles: Guiding Companies with Wisdom and Experience

Even as the Silent Generation steps away from day-to-day business operations, they continue to provide invaluable leadership in board positions. Many successful companies recognize that a well-rounded board includes experienced professionals who have seen industries shift and evolve over time.

Stability and Long-Term Vision

Silent Generation board members bring a steadying presence to corporate governance. Unlike newer executives who may prioritize short-term performance metrics, they advocate for sustainable growth and ethical business practices. Their ability to think long-term—while ensuring financial stability and company reputation—

helps businesses avoid impulsive or overly aggressive decision-making.

Additionally, their knowledge of legal, regulatory, and compliance frameworks is particularly beneficial for organizations operating in highly regulated industries. Having witnessed decades of evolving business laws, they provide guidance on navigating complex regulatory landscapes while upholding ethical standards.

Serving as Ethical Compasses

In an era where corporate social responsibility is under scrutiny, Silent Generation board members often serve as ethical compasses, ensuring that businesses prioritize integrity over short-term profit. Many of them have spent their careers in industries where personal reputation and trust were paramount, making them ideal watchdogs for maintaining corporate accountability.

Their ability to ask the right questions—about business ethics, employee treatment, and corporate transparency—helps protect a company's long-term credibility and public trust.

A Resource for Conflict Resolution

Boards often face internal conflicts, particularly as newer generations bring different priorities to leadership discussions. Silent Generation board members act as mediators, leveraging their experience in handling negotiations, stakeholder management, and leadership transitions. Their ability to de-escalate conflicts and find practical solutions makes them valuable assets to any board.

Why Businesses Should Retain Silent Generation Experts

While some may assume that retirement marks the end of professional contribution, the Silent Generation proves otherwise. Their continued involvement in consulting, mentorship, and board leadership provides businesses with unparalleled experience, wisdom, and institutional stability. Companies that actively retain their expertise benefit from:

- Stronger decision-making frameworks – Leveraging decades of business acumen.
- Smoother leadership transitions – Ensuring younger executives have a foundation of guidance.
- Higher employee engagement – Providing younger workers with access to experienced mentors.

- More ethical business practices – Fostering corporate responsibility and long-term sustainability.

By integrating Silent Generation professionals into consulting, mentorship, and board roles, businesses not only honor their contributions but also set themselves up for long-term success. The knowledge and values they offer are timeless, and their presence ensures that the principles of discipline, responsibility, and strategic thinking remain embedded in the future of work.

The next section will explore practical tools for businesses looking to effectively utilize the Silent Generation's experience before they fully retire, ensuring a seamless transition of knowledge and leadership within organizations.

Practical Tools: Best Ways to Leverage Their Experience Before Retirement

As the Silent Generation transitions out of the workforce, businesses must act strategically to capture and retain their invaluable knowledge before it's lost. These individuals hold decades of industry insights, leadership wisdom, and practical expertise that can benefit both companies and younger employees. Rather than letting this knowledge fade with retirement, organizations should implement structured approaches to ensure that their contributions remain a lasting legacy.

Below are practical tools and strategies that business owners and leaders can use to maximize the Silent Generation's experience before they step away from the workforce entirely.

1. Establish a Formal Knowledge Transfer Program

One of the biggest challenges businesses face when long-term employees retire is the loss of institutional knowledge. While younger employees bring innovation and new perspectives, they often lack the context and experience necessary to navigate industry-specific challenges effectively.

- Create a Knowledge Bank – Develop a structured repository where senior employees document best practices, industry insights, and business processes.
- Encourage Documentation – Ask Silent Generation professionals to record detailed procedures, client relationship histories, and key decision-making frameworks to create a playbook for future employees.
- Conduct Knowledge-Sharing Workshops – Hold monthly roundtables where Silent Generation professionals share their experiences, industry trends, and past challenges with younger employees.

2. Implement Structured Mentorship Programs

Many businesses already have informal mentorship opportunities, but creating structured programs ensures that knowledge transfer happens consistently and effectively.

- Pair Senior Employees with High-Potential Talent – Match Silent Generation employees with younger professionals who demonstrate leadership potential.
- Reverse Mentorship – Encourage cross-generational learning where younger employees teach Silent Generation

professionals about new technologies, digital strategies, and emerging workplace trends.
- Set Clear Objectives – Define mentorship goals, such as leadership development, industry expertise, and communication skills, to ensure both parties benefit from the relationship.
- Create a Mentorship Timeline – Develop a 6-to-12-month roadmap that includes structured learning sessions, case study discussions, and practical exercises to ensure meaningful engagement.

3. Encourage Advisory and Consulting Roles Post-Retirement

Many Silent Generation professionals still want to contribute even after retirement. Offering flexible, part-time consulting or advisory roles allows businesses to retain their expertise without requiring full-time commitments.

- Offer Retired Employees a Consulting Pathway – Provide part-time or on-demand consulting roles where retirees can step in for specific projects or challenges.
- Create an Advisory Board – Invite retired professionals to participate in strategy meetings, industry roundtables, and

decision-making processes without requiring a full-time presence.

- Leverage Their Networks – Many Silent Generation professionals have built extensive business relationships. Engage them in client retention strategies, stakeholder negotiations, and partnership development.

4. Utilize Digital Tools for Ongoing Knowledge Sharing

Given that today's workforce is highly digital, businesses must ensure that the Silent Generation's insights are preserved in accessible and scalable formats.

- Record Video Interviews and Webinars – Capture industry insights, leadership lessons, and success stories through video documentation that employees can refer to in the future.
- Develop an Internal Knowledge Base – Create an intranet or digital library where senior employees can upload training materials, case studies, and leadership advice.
- Encourage Online Discussion Forums – Establish private forums or Slack channels where Silent Generation professionals can participate in ongoing discussions, answer questions, and share advice asynchronously.

5. Design Legacy Projects and Leadership Transition Plans

The transition of leadership is often one of the most delicate aspects of business succession. Organizations can proactively create legacy projects that honor Silent Generation professionals while ensuring that their impact lasts beyond their tenure.

- Establish a Named Leadership Program – Create a mentorship or training initiative named after a retiring leader, reinforcing their influence within the company.
- Document Case Studies and Business Success Stories – Encourage senior employees to share real-life industry challenges and how they were solved, offering valuable insights for the next generation.
- Plan for Succession Early – Ensure that key leadership roles have clear succession plans that incorporate Silent Generation professionals in the transition process.

6. Offer Flexible Transition Plans Instead of Immediate Retirement

Not all Silent Generation professionals want to retire abruptly. Many prefer a gradual transition, where they can reduce hours while still contributing to business operations.

- Implement Phased Retirement Plans – Allow employees to gradually step down from full-time roles instead of an abrupt exit.
- Develop Coaching and Training Opportunities – Engage retirees in short-term leadership coaching and internal training programs.
- Encourage Passion Projects – Some Silent Generation professionals may want to focus on industry advocacy, community outreach, or corporate social responsibility efforts as part of their legacy.

7. Recognize and Celebrate Their Contributions

Acknowledging the dedication and contributions of Silent Generation employees strengthens workplace culture and encourages multi-generational respect.

- Host Retirement Celebrations – Organize a meaningful farewell event that honors their impact, showcases their legacy, and fosters intergenerational appreciation.
- Create an Employee Legacy Wall – Dedicate a section of the workplace (physical or digital) that highlights key accomplishments, quotes, and lessons learned from Silent Generation employees.
- Encourage Peer Recognition – Allow colleagues and direct reports to share personal stories and testimonials about how these senior professionals influenced their careers.

The Silent Generation represents an irreplaceable source of wisdom, stability, and institutional knowledge. Businesses that proactively engage their expertise before retirement will not only benefit from their insights but also ensure a seamless leadership transition and long-term continuity.

By implementing structured mentorship programs, consulting roles, digital knowledge-sharing initiatives, and phased retirement options, organizations can capture the value of the Silent Generation before they step away entirely. These strategies don't just honor the past—they shape the future of the workplace, ensuring that foundational business principles remain strong while evolving to meet modern demands.

But as the Silent Generation gradually exits the workforce, a new challenge emerges: the Baby Boomers, who aren't just retiring—they're redefining what retirement even means. Unlike their predecessors, Boomers didn't just inherit the corporate structures of the past—they expanded them, creating the high-paced, success-driven workplaces we know today. As they transition out of leadership roles, their impact remains undeniable. The question now is: how do businesses adapt to the changing expectations of a generation that shaped the modern workforce?

Chapter 2: Baby Boomers – The Workaholics Turned Mentors

"Choose a job you love, and you will never have to work a day in your life."

— Confucius

Q: "What does success look like to you?"

A: "Success is about working hard, climbing the ladder, and proving yourself. I was raised to believe that if you put in the effort, you'll be rewarded. A long career with one company, a strong reputation, and the ability to retire on my own terms—those are the things that matter. If people recognize your hard work and you've built something to be proud of, you've made it."

The Baby Boomer generation, born between 1946 and 1964, has played a defining role in shaping modern corporate culture. Their approach to work, leadership, and professional success has left a lasting imprint on industries across the globe. Raised in a time of economic prosperity, post-war expansion, and rapid technological advancements, Boomers grew up believing in the value of hard work, discipline, and loyalty to an organization. For decades, they have been the driving force behind corporate growth, often working long hours, climbing the ranks, and solidifying the structures that define many businesses today.

Unlike their predecessors in the Silent Generation, who adhered to a strict sense of duty and hierarchy, Boomers actively pursued career advancement and financial success. They saw work as a means to an identity, often associating their self-worth with their professional achievements. Boomers value stability but also seek opportunities for reinvention. This generation is known for its competitive spirit, goal-oriented mindset, and commitment to organizational growth. They have historically been the first ones in the office and the last to leave, believing that dedication and perseverance would be rewarded with promotions, financial security, and respect in their industries.

As leaders, Boomers prioritized structure, order, and results. Many of today's corporate traditions—such as hierarchical leadership models, performance evaluations, and the concept of climbing the corporate ladder—can be traced back to the values and workplace norms established by this generation. Their leadership style is

Chapter 2: Baby Boomers – The Workaholics Turned Mentors

authoritative yet mentorship-driven, often shaped by their experiences of rising through the ranks. They believe in earning your place through experience and hard work, which has both inspired and frustrated younger generations who value collaboration, flexibility, and rapid career progression.

However, as they near retirement, Baby Boomers find themselves at a crossroads. The workplace they once dominated is evolving at a pace faster than they ever imagined. Digital transformation, remote work, and younger generations' demands for work-life balance challenge many of their long-held beliefs about how work should be structured and executed. The very principles that made them successful—dedication, long hours, and in-person collaboration—are being questioned by a new workforce that prioritizes efficiency, innovation, and technological integration over tradition.

This transition hasn't been seamless. Many Boomers struggle to adapt to remote work environments where they can't rely on face-to-face interactions to maintain team cohesion and enforce accountability. Others wrestle with new technology, automation, and digital platforms that seem to disrupt the systems they spent decades refining. At the same time, the rise of Millennial and Gen Z leaders has introduced leadership styles that emphasize collaboration over hierarchy, purpose-driven work over profit-driven goals, and work-life balance over long hours. This shift has, at times, led to friction between Boomers and younger employees, as differing values and work expectations create misunderstandings and resistance to change.

Yet, despite these challenges, Baby Boomers remain an invaluable asset to today's workforce. Their depth of experience, industry knowledge, and leadership wisdom provide a foundation that companies cannot afford to lose. As the corporate world continues to evolve, businesses must find ways to retain and integrate the expertise of Boomers while also adapting to the expectations of younger workers. The key lies in striking a balance—leveraging their experience without resisting progress and ensuring that their knowledge is passed down in meaningful ways.

In the following sections, we will explore how Baby Boomers have influenced corporate culture and leadership, the struggles they face in adapting to remote work and digital transformation, and the practical strategies businesses can implement to retain their knowledge while integrating modern workplace practices. By understanding their perspective and finding ways to merge traditional values with modern expectations, organizations can create workplaces that honor past achievements while embracing the future.

Their Impact on Corporate Culture and Leadership

The Baby Boomer generation has had a profound impact on corporate culture and leadership. As one of the largest generational cohorts in history, their presence in the workforce shaped the modern business environment in ways that continue to influence organizations today. From work ethic and leadership philosophy to organizational structures and workplace norms, Boomers established many of the systems that define professional life.

Shaping Corporate Culture: The Boomers' Influence

Corporate culture as we know it today was largely molded by the Baby Boomer generation. Entering the workforce in the 1960s and 1970s, Boomers benefited from post-war economic expansion and the rise of large corporations that promoted structured career growth and long-term job security. As a result, their work culture emphasized:

- Loyalty and Long-Term Commitment – Many Boomers joined companies expecting to stay for decades, climbing the corporate ladder in a structured manner. They valued stability, pension plans, and job security, which led to workplace cultures that prioritized employee retention and long-term career development.
- Hierarchical Structures – Boomers entered organizations that favored clear chains of command, where decisions flowed

from top to bottom. Promotions were based on tenure, and leadership was often seen as something to be earned over time.
- Performance-Based Recognition – Hard work and dedication were seen as the keys to success. Corporate cultures became increasingly competitive and meritocratic, rewarding those who put in long hours, demonstrated strong performance, and adhered to company expectations.
- Work as a Defining Identity – Unlike later generations that seek work-life balance, Boomers viewed work as a core part of their identity. Success was often measured by career achievements, promotions, and financial security rather than personal fulfillment.

The Rise of the Traditional Leadership Model

As Boomers advanced in their careers, they introduced a leadership style that emphasized authority, expertise, and structured management. Their approach to leadership had several key characteristics:

1. Hierarchical Leadership

Boomer leaders traditionally embraced a top-down leadership model, where decision-making was centralized, and authority was respected. This approach was influenced by the military-style leadership that many of their parents (Silent Generation) experienced during World War II.

- Clear Roles and Responsibilities – Employees had well-defined roles, with promotions occurring through tenure and proven results.
- Chain of Command – Leadership structures were rigid, with senior executives holding the most power and mid-level managers ensuring directives were followed.
- Limited Direct Access to Leadership – Employees were expected to follow protocol, and report issues up the chain rather than engaging in open collaboration.

While this structure created organizational stability, it also led to rigidity, making it challenging for younger employees to introduce innovative ideas or disrupt traditional workflows.

2. Emphasis on Work Ethic and Productivity

Boomers grew up in a time when hard work equaled success. As leaders, they expected employees to demonstrate:

- Dedication and Commitment – Employees were encouraged to put in extra hours and prioritize work over personal life.
- Professionalism and Formality – Business attire, structured meetings, and formal communication were standard.

- Results-Oriented Performance – Employees were judged by measurable outcomes, and promotions were often tied to achieving high-performance metrics.

While this work ethic contributed to strong corporate growth, it also led to high stress levels, burnout, and a culture that sometimes prioritized work over employee well-being.

3. Competitive, Results-Driven Leadership

Boomer leaders fostered a workplace culture that thrived on competition and performance-based rewards. While this created ambitious environments that pushed organizations forward, it also:

- Encouraged Individual Success Over Teamwork – Many companies prioritized individual accomplishments, leading to a less collaborative environment.
- Created Pressure to Conform to Corporate Norms – Employees were expected to adhere to company culture rather than challenge or reshape it.
- Limited Work-Life Balance – The expectation of long hours led to high stress levels and work-centric lifestyles.

Their Legacy in Corporate Leadership

Despite the challenges associated with hierarchical leadership, the impact of Baby Boomers remains evident in today's business world. Their mentorship, structured corporate governance, and strategic decision-making skills have left a lasting imprint, influencing leadership training programs and executive management.

However, as workplaces shift toward more collaborative, flexible, and innovative cultures, Boomers have had to adapt to new leadership expectations and evolving corporate environments. Many organizations now seek to balance the discipline and professionalism of Boomer-led structures with the creativity and agility demanded by younger generations.

The Modern Evolution of Boomer Leadership

As Millennials and Gen Z take on leadership roles, companies are seeing a shift from authoritarian to collaborative management styles. Yet, Boomer leaders are still integral in guiding businesses through transitions, offering:

- Institutional Knowledge – Their deep understanding of industry evolution provides historical context for business decisions.

- Mentorship and Coaching – Many Boomers have taken on mentoring roles, helping younger professionals navigate their careers.
- Strategic Oversight – Their experience allows them to offer risk-aware guidance, ensuring stability during economic fluctuations.

To remain relevant in today's workforce, Boomer leaders are learning to adapt by embracing technology, fostering collaboration, and rethinking workplace structures to meet the expectations of younger employees.

The Baby Boomer generation played an undeniable role in shaping corporate culture and leadership. Their emphasis on hard work, structured career paths, and competitive success built many of the institutions we see today. However, as the workplace continues to evolve, businesses must find ways to blend Boomer leadership values with modern workplace innovations to create organizations that honor tradition while embracing the future.

The next section will explore the challenges Baby Boomers face in adapting to remote work, digital transformation, and younger leadership styles—a shift that is redefining the very structures they helped create.

Struggles with Remote Work, Digital Transformation, and Younger Leadership

The rise of remote work, digital transformation, and younger leadership has created a seismic shift in workplace dynamics—one that Baby Boomers have found particularly challenging to navigate. Having built their careers in environments where face-to-face interaction, rigid corporate hierarchies, and traditional work ethics were the norm, they now find themselves adjusting to a world where work is increasingly flexible, virtual, and decentralized. This transformation has not been without friction, as Boomers attempt to reconcile the principles they've spent decades refining with a new, fast-paced digital workplace culture.

The Remote Work Dilemma

For much of their careers, Baby Boomers operated under the assumption that being physically present in the workplace was essential to productivity and success. Offices were seen as the hub of professional activity, where work got done through in-person meetings, direct supervision, and interpersonal collaboration. In this structure, seniority and tenure were valued, and success was often measured by hours spent at the office rather than results alone.

The COVID-19 pandemic accelerated the global shift to remote work, and while many businesses have embraced hybrid or fully remote models, Boomers have struggled with the loss of traditional workplace structures. Challenges include:

- A Sense of Disconnection – Many Boomers feel isolated when working remotely, as they thrive on in-person networking, spontaneous conversations, and office culture.
- Trust and Accountability – Having grown up in workplaces where visibility equated to productivity, some Boomers find it difficult to trust that work is being done effectively in a remote setting.
- Tech Fatigue – Virtual collaboration tools like Zoom, Slack, and project management software have created a steep learning curve for some Boomers, who are more accustomed to face-to-face communication and email correspondence.
- Managing Remote Teams – Leading a team remotely requires a different skill set than managing in-person, with an emphasis on asynchronous communication, digital engagement, and performance-based trust rather than physical oversight.

While some Boomers have adapted successfully, others feel left behind in a workplace that now prioritizes results over rigid schedules, values digital interaction over in-person meetings, and rewards efficiency over time spent at a desk.

The Challenges of Digital Transformation

Boomers are no strangers to technological advancements—they witnessed the rise of personal computers, email, and the internet—but today's digital transformation is happening at an unprecedented pace. The integration of AI, automation, cloud computing, and data-driven decision-making has redefined business operations, often leaving Baby Boomers feeling overwhelmed by the constant need to relearn and adapt.

Some of the biggest challenges include:
- Adapting to Rapid Technological Change – Unlike Millennials and Gen Z, who grew up in a digital-first world, Boomers often find themselves playing catch-up with new software, collaboration tools, and AI-driven workflows.
- Resisting Automation – Many Boomers built their careers on manual processes and hands-on experience. The replacement of human decision-making with automation and AI can feel like a threat to their expertise and job security.
- Lack of Digital Confidence – While Boomers are fully capable of learning new technology, some may experience imposter syndrome when navigating tech-heavy environments dominated by younger, more tech-savvy colleagues.
- Communication Gaps – The shift from phone calls and in-person meetings to Slack messages and video conferences

has changed how communication happens, often leading to misunderstandings and frustration.

To bridge the gap, organizations must offer targeted digital upskilling programs for Baby Boomers, providing them with personalized training, mentorship in digital fluency, and opportunities to apply new technologies in a low-pressure setting. Rather than expecting Boomers to immediately adapt, companies should integrate them into change management initiatives, allowing them to contribute their expertise while learning new systems at a sustainable pace.

The Shift in Leadership: Navigating Younger Generations in Power

Perhaps one of the most difficult transitions for Baby Boomers is adjusting to a workforce where Millennials and Gen Z are now in leadership roles. Many Boomers have spent decades climbing the corporate ladder, only to find that leadership styles and workplace expectations have drastically shifted under younger generations.

Key differences include:
- Hierarchical vs. Collaborative Leadership – Boomers traditionally value top-down leadership, where authority is earned through experience and tenure. Younger leaders favor flat organizational structures, where employees are encouraged to challenge ideas and collaborate across levels.

- Work-Life Balance Expectations – Whereas Boomers often equate hard work with long hours, Millennials and Gen Z prioritize efficiency, well-being, and flexible schedules.
- Feedback and Recognition – Boomers were accustomed to annual performance reviews, whereas younger leaders practice real-time feedback, coaching, and public recognition.
- Diversity and Inclusion Priorities – While Boomers value merit-based advancement, younger leaders place greater emphasis on equity, representation, and cultural inclusivity in leadership decisions.

For Boomers who have been at the top of corporate hierarchies, taking direction from younger leaders can feel like an unsettling power shift. Some struggle with being managed by individuals with fewer years of experience, while others find it difficult to adjust to leadership styles that prioritize emotional intelligence, adaptability, and inclusivity over traditional command-and-control approaches.

Overcoming Generational Friction in the Workplace

While these changes can create friction, businesses must find ways to integrate Boomers into the modern workforce without dismissing their expertise. Strategies include:
- Reverse Mentorship Programs – Pairing Boomers with younger leaders to exchange knowledge: Boomers share industry

expertise while younger leaders provide insights into digital trends and modern leadership techniques.

- Flexible Leadership Roles – Encouraging Boomers to transition into advisory or mentorship roles, where they can guide younger leaders without feeling sidelined.
- Bridging Communication Styles – Encouraging multi-generational teams to blend traditional leadership principles with modern, people-centric management styles.
- Encouraging Open Dialogue – Creating safe spaces for cross-generational conversations, where Boomers can express concerns and learn about new workplace expectations without judgment.

The challenges Baby Boomers face in the modern workforce are real, but they are not insurmountable. While remote work, digital transformation, and younger leadership have reshaped business norms, Boomers still have immense value to offer. The key to successfully integrating them into today's workforce lies in education, adaptation, and mutual respect—ensuring that Boomers feel empowered rather than displaced, and that businesses benefit from both their experience and the innovation of younger generations.

By fostering an environment where knowledge is exchanged rather than dismissed, companies can create stronger, more inclusive workplaces that honor the contributions of every generation.

Practical Tools: How to Retain Their Knowledge While Integrating Modern Workplace Practices

As Baby Boomers transition out of leadership roles and into retirement, organizations face a significant challenge: how to capture and retain their invaluable knowledge while integrating modern workplace practices. Boomers have spent decades refining processes, building relationships, and shaping corporate culture, and losing their expertise without proper transition planning can create gaps in institutional knowledge, leadership stability, and workforce cohesion.

Businesses that proactively implement knowledge-sharing initiatives, mentorship programs, and strategic technology integration will not only honor the contributions of Boomers but also create a more sustainable, adaptable workforce that leverages both traditional expertise and modern innovation. Below are practical tools to help retain Baby Boomer knowledge while ensuring smooth integration into evolving workplace dynamics.

1. Create a Structured Knowledge Transfer Program

One of the most significant risks of Boomer retirements is the loss of industry knowledge that isn't documented or easily accessible. To prevent this, businesses should establish a formal knowledge transfer framework that ensures key insights, strategies, and expertise are passed down to younger employees.

How to Implement:
- Develop an Institutional Knowledge Database – Create an internal, cloud-based repository where senior employees can upload best practices, case studies, decision-making frameworks, and industry insights.
- Document Critical Processes – Encourage Boomers to record step-by-step guides, client relationship histories, and lessons learned from past challenges.
- Conduct Exit Interviews and Legacy Roundtables – Before retirement, facilitate discussions where Boomers share insights on leadership, crisis management, and strategic planning with key successors.

2. Establish Cross-Generational Mentorship Programs

Boomers bring decades of experience, while younger employees bring technical fluency and fresh perspectives. Businesses should leverage reverse mentorship programs to facilitate cross-generational knowledge exchange.

How to Implement:

- Pair Senior Employees with Rising Leaders – Assign Boomers as mentors to high-potential Millennials and Gen Z employees to foster leadership development.
- Create Reverse Mentorship Opportunities – Encourage younger employees to teach Boomers digital skills, AI-driven tools, and emerging workplace technologies.
- Set Defined Learning Goals – Establish mentorship objectives that balance technical upskilling for Boomers and leadership refinement for younger employees.

3. Leverage Technology to Preserve and Share Expertise

Given the increasing reliance on AI, cloud-based tools, and automation, businesses should integrate digital knowledge-sharing systems to ensure that Boomers' insights remain accessible beyond their retirement.

How to Implement:

- Record Video Interviews and Webinars – Capture key leaders discussing business strategies, client relationship management, and industry trends.
- Create an Internal Podcast or Blog – Boomers can contribute articles, interviews, and discussions on company history, strategic planning, and leadership philosophies.

- **Use AI-Powered Knowledge Management Systems** – Implement digital archives where employees can search for solutions, historical insights, and strategic decisions made by Boomers.

4. Develop Leadership Transition Plans

Succession planning is essential to ensuring a smooth transition from Boomer leadership to Millennial and Gen Z executives. A well-structured plan prevents disruption and allows for an overlapping period where senior leaders gradually shift responsibilities.

How to Implement:
- Create a Leadership Shadowing Program – Allow future leaders to shadow Boomers in key meetings, negotiations, and decision-making processes.
- Gradually Transfer Responsibilities – Implement a phased leadership transition, where Boomers delegate tasks over 12–24 months rather than stepping away suddenly.
- Maintain Advisory Roles – Offer Boomers part-time consulting or board positions to keep them engaged while allowing younger leaders to take the reins.

5. Encourage Inter-Generational Collaboration

Workplaces thrive when generations learn from each other rather than operating in silos. Encouraging collaborative projects and team diversity fosters a culture where Boomer expertise is embedded into modern workplace innovation.

How to Implement:
- Form Cross-Generational Task Forces – Create teams that include Boomers, Gen X, Millennials, and Gen Z to work on company-wide initiatives.
- Encourage Knowledge Exchange Through Storytelling – Host company forums, roundtable discussions, or fireside chats where Boomers share experiences and lessons with younger employees.
- Recognize Multi-Generational Team Achievements – Promote and reward projects where multiple generations contribute to success.

6. Adapt Workplace Practices Without Alienating Boomers

As businesses integrate remote work, AI, and digital transformation, it's crucial to support Boomers in adapting to these changes rather than forcing abrupt transitions.

How to Implement:

- Offer Personalized Digital Training – Provide customized workshops on digital collaboration tools, automation software, and data-driven decision-making.
- Introduce Gradual Change Management Strategies – Implement workplace adjustments in phases, allowing Boomers to adapt to new expectations over time.
- Respect Traditional Strengths – Balance modernization with legacy leadership principles, ensuring that discipline, accountability, and institutional knowledge remain part of workplace culture.

7. Honor and Celebrate Boomer Contributions

Recognizing the legacy of Boomers is critical to maintaining morale, workplace culture, and cross-generational respect. Their contributions should be honored not just upon retirement but throughout their careers.

How to Implement:

- Create a Hall of Legacy – Establish a digital or physical space recognizing Boomers' impact, featuring their leadership achievements, career milestones, and contributions.
- Host Legacy Dinners or Ceremonies – Organize events celebrating key retirees, ensuring that they feel appreciated as they transition out of leadership.

- Offer Named Mentorship and Leadership Programs – Design programs bearing the names of impactful Boomer leaders, ensuring that their influence continues to shape future professionals.

Baby Boomers have spent decades shaping industries, leading organizations, and establishing business practices that remain relevant today. While the modern workplace is evolving, their expertise remains an invaluable asset. Businesses that proactively capture their knowledge, integrate structured mentorship programs, and provide adaptive leadership transition strategies will create workforces that blend experience with innovation, tradition with modernization, and mentorship with continuous learning.

By honoring Boomer contributions while embracing new workplace expectations, organizations can build sustainable, multi-generational teams that thrive in today's dynamic business landscape.

But as Boomers step back from leadership, Gen X is stepping up. Often overlooked between two much larger generations, Gen X has spent its career adapting—learning from Boomers while paving the way for Millennials. Unlike their predecessors, Gen X leaders reject rigid hierarchies and embrace autonomy, problem-solving, and efficiency. If Boomers built the corporate world as we know it, Gen X is the generation that questioned it—challenging outdated structures and redefining what leadership looks like in today's workforce.

Chapter 3: Gen X – The No-BS Managers

"No one is going to give you the education you need to overthrow them."

— Assata Shakur

Q: "What does success look like to you?"

A: "Success is about independence. It's not just about money or titles—it's about having the freedom to live life on your own terms. I don't want to be micromanaged or stuck in a job where I have no control. Success means having options—financial security, work-life balance, and the ability to walk away if something isn't working. I don't need constant praise; I just want to get the job done and be left alone to do it."

Born between 1965 and 1980, Generation X occupies a unique and often overlooked position in the workforce. Sandwiched between the traditionalist Baby Boomers and the progressive Millennials, Gen Xers have had to adapt to changing workplace expectations while forging their own leadership style. They are often described as the "middle child" of the workforce, balancing the pragmatism and work ethic of Boomers with the innovation and adaptability of Millennials.

Gen X grew up during a time of shifting societal norms and economic turbulence. They witnessed the decline of lifelong job security, the rise of dual-income households, and the early impact of technology on the workplace. As a result, they developed a self-sufficient, resourceful, and results-driven mindset that sets them apart from other generations. Unlike Baby Boomers, who embraced hierarchical structures, and Millennials, who thrive in collaborative environments, Gen X values autonomy and directness. They are not interested in unnecessary meetings, corporate fluff, or micromanagement. Instead, they prefer to get the job done efficiently and with minimal interference.

Despite their significant contributions to the workplace, Gen X is often overshadowed by the larger, more vocal Baby Boomer and Millennial generations. However, their role as a bridge between these two dominant cohorts is critical. They understand and respect the hard work and commitment of Boomers, but they also appreciate the flexibility and technological savvy of Millennials. This ability to adapt and connect across generations makes Gen X invaluable in today's workforce.

In recent years, many Gen Xers have ascended to leadership roles, where they have made their mark with a no-nonsense approach to management. Unlike previous generations, who may have emphasized loyalty and tenure, Gen X leaders prioritize competence, results, and efficiency. They believe that work should be evaluated based on outcomes rather than time spent in the office, making them some of the strongest advocates for performance-based work cultures.

However, this generational shift in leadership has not been without challenges. Gen X managers often find themselves caught between Boomers who are reluctant to relinquish control and Millennials who demand more flexibility, feedback, and purpose in their work. As a result, they must constantly navigate conflicting expectations, balance tradition with innovation, and refine their management approach to accommodate the evolving workforce.

One of the defining characteristics of Gen X is their strong sense of independence. Many members of this generation were latchkey kids, growing up with working parents and a high degree of personal responsibility from a young age. This background shaped their preference for autonomy and dislike for micromanagement. Unlike Millennials, who thrive on constant feedback and collaboration, Gen Xers prefer to be given a goal and left to figure out the best way to achieve it. They take pride in their ability to problem-solve without excessive oversight, making them highly effective in environments that reward self-direction and efficiency.

Despite their preference for independence, Gen Xers are not disconnected or disengaged managers. In fact, they excel at mentorship and coaching, largely because they understand the struggles of both Boomers and Millennials. They value competence and expect employees to take ownership of their work, but they are also willing to offer guidance when needed—without excessive hand-holding. Their leadership style is straightforward and pragmatic, focusing on clear expectations, direct communication, and tangible results.

As workplaces continue to evolve, Gen X leaders are playing a crucial role in modernizing management practices. They are early adopters of flexible work arrangements, understanding that results matter more than rigid schedules. At the same time, they maintain a strong sense of accountability, ensuring that employees meet performance expectations without relying on outdated, authoritarian leadership tactics.

This chapter will explore the defining traits of Gen X as independent problem-solvers, their ability to bridge the gap between Boomers and Millennials, and practical strategies for businesses to leverage their leadership strengths. By the end of this chapter, you will have a clearer understanding of why Gen X is essential in today's workforce and how organizations can maximize their impact in leadership and management roles.

The Independent Problem-Solvers Who Dislike Micromanagement

Generation X, often referred to as the "latchkey generation," grew up in a world where independence wasn't just encouraged—it was a necessity. Many Gen Xers were raised by dual-income or single-parent households, meaning they often had to take care of themselves, complete homework without supervision, and develop a strong sense of self-reliance from an early age. This upbringing directly influenced their professional mindset, making them some of the most resourceful and independent problem-solvers in the workforce today.

Unlike Boomers, who value hierarchical structures, and Millennials, who seek constant collaboration, Gen X thrives on autonomy. They prefer to be given a goal and the freedom to determine the best way to achieve it. Micromanagement is not only frustrating for them—it's demotivating. They view excessive oversight as a lack of trust, and nothing stifles their productivity more than feeling like they are being constantly monitored or second-guessed.

The Root of Their Independent Work Ethic

Several factors shaped Gen X's preference for independence and dislike for micromanagement:

- Self-Sufficiency from a Young Age: Growing up with more responsibility than previous generations, they learned to solve problems on their own without waiting for guidance.
- The Rise of Technology in the Workplace: Many Gen Xers adapted to rapid technological advancements during their careers, learning new skills on their own as industries evolved.
- A Shift Away from Corporate Loyalty: Witnessing economic instability and layoffs in the 1980s and 1990s, Gen X became skeptical of company loyalty and focused on developing transferable skills that would allow them to succeed anywhere.
- Pragmatism Over Office Politics: Unlike Boomers who climbed corporate ladders through networking and Millennials who prioritize workplace culture, Gen Xers believe that results matter more than face time.

Why Micromanagement Frustrates Gen X Employees and Leaders

One of the quickest ways to lose the engagement of a Gen X employee or leader is to micromanage them. They believe that if they've been hired or promoted to do a job, they should be trusted to execute it without constant oversight. Micromanagement disrupts their workflow and creates unnecessary inefficiencies.

Some of the key reasons why Gen X resists micromanagement include:

- It Undermines Their Expertise: Many Gen X professionals have spent decades refining their skills. Having someone oversee every detail of their work can feel insulting and counterproductive.
- It Slows Down Decision-Making: Gen X leaders are known for making quick, informed decisions. When every choice requires approval, it creates unnecessary bottlenecks.
- It Reduces Innovation: When employees are constantly monitored, they become less likely to take initiative or experiment with new approaches.
- It Erodes Trust: Gen X values workplace relationships built on trust and respect. Micromanagement signals to them that their employer or leader does not trust their judgment.

How Gen X Approaches Problem-Solving

Gen X thrives in environments that encourage solution-oriented thinking. They approach problem-solving with a blend of practicality, adaptability, and efficiency. Unlike Millennials, who might seek collaborative brainstorming sessions, or Boomers, who rely on traditional corporate frameworks, Gen X prefers to assess the issue independently, develop a logical solution, and take action.

Their problem-solving approach often follows these key steps:

- Assess the Situation Quickly: Gen X leaders don't waste time overanalyzing. They identify the core issue, eliminate distractions, and focus on the problem at hand.
- Leverage Past Experiences: Having worked through multiple economic downturns, technological shifts, and corporate restructures, they apply lessons learned from the past to current challenges.
- Take Initiative and Ownership: Gen X employees don't wait for permission to fix problems. They take proactive measures to address issues before they escalate.
- Adapt to Changing Circumstances: Because they've witnessed constant industry evolution, Gen X is comfortable making adjustments on the fly.
- Communicate Only When Necessary: Unlike younger generations that rely on group chats and frequent check-ins, Gen X prefers direct and efficient communication to keep projects moving forward.

Gen X as Leaders: Encouraging Independence in Others

As managers, Gen X leaders avoid micromanagement themselves, because they dislike it just as much as they did when they were employees. Instead of closely monitoring their teams, they focus on empowering their employees to succeed on their own.

Their leadership style is centered around the following principles:

- Trust Over Control: Gen X managers delegate tasks with confidence and expect employees to take ownership.
- Results-Oriented Management: Instead of tracking every small action, they measure performance based on outcomes, efficiency, and impact.
- Encouraging Self-Sufficiency: They expect employees to problem-solve on their own before coming to them for help.
- Providing Guidance, Not Micromanagement: If an employee needs direction, Gen X managers prefer to offer coaching and mentorship, rather than checking in constantly.

One of the reasons Gen X managers are so effective is their ability to create balance. Unlike Boomers, who may default to hierarchical oversight, or Millennials, who thrive on collaboration, Gen X leaders find a middle ground between independence and support. They value autonomy but remain available for guidance when necessary.

How Companies Can Support Gen X's Strengths

For organizations that want to maximize the potential of Gen X employees and leaders, it's important to create an environment that aligns with their work preferences. Here's how businesses can support them:

1. Offer Autonomy and Flexibility
- Allow Gen X employees to work independently without excessive oversight.
- Provide flexible work arrangements, including hybrid and remote options, to accommodate their preference for self-management.

2. Minimize Unnecessary Meetings and Bureaucracy
- Avoid scheduling meetings that could be replaced with quick emails or written updates.
- Streamline approval processes so they can make decisions efficiently.

3. Recognize and Reward Results, Not Just Presence
- Instead of tracking hours worked, focus on measurable contributions and project success.
- Recognize problem-solving abilities and initiative, which Gen X highly values.

4. Implement Direct and Efficient Communication

- Use clear, concise communication methods that allow them to process information quickly.
- Avoid overly complicated collaboration platforms and focus on practical tools that enhance productivity.

5. Provide Growth Opportunities Without Excessive Oversight

- Offer leadership development programs that align with their independent mindset.
- Encourage participation in strategic decision-making, giving them the ability to influence company direction.

Gen X professionals bring a refreshing level of pragmatism, self-sufficiency, and efficiency to the workplace. Their dislike for micromanagement isn't about resistance to leadership—it's about their desire to be trusted to do their jobs well. Companies that recognize and support this independence will benefit from their problem-solving skills, adaptability, and strong leadership qualities.

As businesses evolve, leveraging the strengths of Gen X's no-nonsense management style will be key to fostering a balanced, results-driven, and self-sufficient workforce. Rather than stifling their independence with excessive oversight, companies should embrace their ability to get things done with minimal interference—because when Gen X thrives, so does the organization.

How They Bridge the Gap Between Boomers and Millennials

Generation X, often referred to as the "middle child" of the workforce, plays a critical role in bridging the gap between Baby Boomers and Millennials. They serve as the balancing force between two very different generations—one that built the foundations of corporate structures and another that is reshaping them entirely. While Boomers value hierarchy, stability, and in-person communication, Millennials prioritize flexibility, innovation, and digital fluency. Gen Xers, positioned between these two groups, act as translators, negotiators, and adaptors, blending traditional work values with modern workplace expectations.

The Gen X Advantage: Understanding Both Sides

Unlike Baby Boomers, who spent much of their careers working under a structured, top-down leadership model, and Millennials, who are accustomed to collaborative, tech-driven workplaces, Gen X grew up adapting to both. They have a unique ability to understand and appreciate the work ethic of Boomers while also embracing the innovative mindset of Millennials. This duality allows them to:

- Respect the experience of Boomers while recognizing that traditional methods must evolve.

- Understand the digital-first approach of Millennials while ensuring that core business principles remain intact.
- Act as mentors who help younger employees navigate corporate structures while guiding older employees through technological advancements.

The Workplace as a Generational Battleground

Boomers and Millennials, despite working side by side, often have vastly different perspectives on work. Some of the most common generational conflicts in the workplace include:

- Work Ethic & Productivity: Boomers equate hard work with long hours, while Millennials prioritize work-life balance and efficiency.
- Communication Styles: Boomers prefer face-to-face meetings, while Millennials favor digital communication like Slack, email, and video calls.
- Career Progression: Boomers value loyalty and tenure, expecting promotions through experience and seniority, while Millennials expect rapid career advancement based on performance and skill development.
- Technology & Change Management: Boomers often struggle with rapid technological changes, while Millennials expect constant digital innovation and adaptability.

Gen X, having experienced both worlds, is uniquely positioned to mediate these differences. They act as the translators between tradition and transformation, ensuring that businesses evolve without alienating employees from different generations.

How Gen X Bridges the Workplace Divide

1. Translating Boomer Work Values into Millennial Expectations

Boomers built careers in a work environment defined by hierarchy, stability, and corporate loyalty. Their belief in "paying your dues" contrasts sharply with Millennials' desire for immediate impact and career acceleration. Gen X leaders understand both perspectives and help bridge this divide by:

- Encouraging structured mentorship programs where Boomers pass down knowledge in a way that aligns with Millennials' expectations for professional development.
- Explaining the value of long-term career growth while advocating for Millennials' need for continuous learning, skill development, and leadership opportunities.
- Reinforcing the importance of work-life balance to Boomers while also instilling a strong work ethic in Millennials.

2. Balancing Traditional & Digital Work Cultures

As the first generation to fully embrace both analog and digital workplaces, Gen Xers are natural tech translators. They understand the importance of in-person collaboration, which Boomers prefer, while also recognizing that digital transformation is essential for businesses to remain competitive in a Millennial and Gen Z-driven economy.

Gen X managers can:
- Encourage Boomers to adopt digital tools without overwhelming them, demonstrating how technology enhances, rather than replaces, traditional work structures.
- Help Millennials understand the importance of face-to-face interaction in building long-term professional relationships, client trust, and leadership presence.
- Integrate hybrid work models that satisfy both generations, balancing remote flexibility with the structured, in-person collaboration that Boomers value.

3. Shaping Leadership Styles that Work for All Generations

Gen X managers have witnessed the transition from top-down, command-and-control leadership to collaborative, people-centric leadership. Unlike Boomers, who often led through authority and tenure, and Millennials, who prefer inclusive decision-making, Gen X strikes a balance between the two.

Key ways Gen X adapts leadership for both generations:
- For Boomers: They provide clear direction and structured decision-making, ensuring that experience and seniority are still respected.
- For Millennials: They offer flexibility, open communication, and continuous feedback, recognizing that career development should be dynamic.
- For Businesses: They focus on results over process, ensuring that workplaces value both performance and work-life balance.

4. Bridging Generational Communication Styles

Miscommunication is one of the biggest sources of intergenerational workplace tension. Boomers prefer formal emails and in-person meetings, while Millennials lean toward instant messaging and asynchronous collaboration. Gen X understands both preferences and facilitates effective communication by:

- Encouraging Boomers to embrace real-time collaboration tools without sacrificing professionalism.
- Teaching Millennials the importance of clear, concise, and structured communication in business settings.

- Promoting a blended communication strategy where different generations use the right tools for the right purpose (e.g., Zoom for remote meetings, Slack for quick updates, and face-to-face for critical conversations).

5. Advocating for a Results-Driven Work Environment

Boomers measure productivity by time spent at the office, while Millennials measure productivity by impact and efficiency. Gen X finds middle ground by shifting the focus away from where or how work gets done to what is actually achieved.

- They champion remote work policies that allow flexibility without sacrificing accountability.
- They advocate for performance-based evaluations, ensuring that both Boomers and Millennials feel valued based on contributions rather than outdated corporate metrics.
- They promote continuous professional development, ensuring that both younger and older employees stay competitive in a fast-changing business landscape.

Why Businesses Need Gen X as the Workforce Evolves

As Millennials become the largest working demographic and Boomers retire, Gen X remains a stabilizing force. Their ability to blend corporate tradition with modern workplace innovation makes them indispensable in leadership roles. Businesses that recognize and leverage Gen X's strengths will:

- Reduce generational conflicts by fostering understanding and collaboration.
- Improve workplace efficiency through practical leadership and streamlined communication.
- Retain institutional knowledge while adapting to modern work expectations.
- Create workplaces that are inclusive, adaptive, and results-driven.

Gen X is the missing link between two workplace extremes—the structured world of Boomers and the flexible, fast-moving mindset of Millennials. Their ability to speak both languages, respect both perspectives, and implement balanced workplace strategies makes them uniquely positioned to drive success in multigenerational teams.

Organizations that tap into Gen X's pragmatism, adaptability, and leadership experience will find that they not only bridge the generational divide but also create a work culture where experience and innovation work together—rather than against each other.

Practical Tools: Effective Leadership Strategies and Engagement Techniques for Gen X

Gen X leaders bring a unique mix of independence, pragmatism, and adaptability to the workplace. Positioned between Baby Boomers and Millennials, they have refined a leadership style that is results-driven, flexible, and highly efficient. Unlike Boomers, who may lean toward hierarchical leadership, or Millennials, who thrive on collaborative decision-making, Gen X finds a balanced approach—one that emphasizes accountability without micromanagement and fosters engagement without excessive oversight.

For businesses to maximize the potential of Gen X leaders, they must adopt strategic leadership development tools, engagement techniques, and workplace policies that align with Gen X values. Below are practical tools and strategies that organizations can implement to leverage Gen X leadership strengths effectively.

1. Empowerment Through Autonomy

Gen X thrives when they are given the freedom to execute their work without unnecessary interference. Unlike Millennials, who seek continuous feedback and collaboration, and Boomers, who value structured oversight, Gen X leaders prefer a results-oriented, hands-off approach.

How to Implement:

- Set Clear Goals, Then Step Back – Define objectives, not methods. Give Gen X leaders the space to determine how to achieve results.
- Eliminate Unnecessary Meetings – Allow for asynchronous communication where possible. Gen X managers prefer direct, concise updates rather than excessive status meetings.
- Trust-Based Performance Metrics – Measure success based on outcomes and deliverables, rather than micromanaging the process.

2. Leverage Their Pragmatic, No-Nonsense Leadership Style

Gen X leaders are known for their straightforward, no-BS approach to management. They value efficiency, direct communication, and practicality over corporate politics or unnecessary complexity.

How to Implement:

- Encourage Direct, Transparent Communication – Minimize bureaucratic layers and corporate jargon. Gen X appreciates clear, honest discussions without sugarcoating.
- Promote Problem-Solving Over Process-Obsessing – Gen X leaders thrive when they can focus on solutions rather than rigid policies.

- Avoid Overly Complex Systems – Simplify workflows and approvals so that Gen X managers can act quickly without red tape.

3. Provide Professional Growth Without Micromanagement

Gen X employees prioritize career development, but they are also self-directed learners who prefer on-the-job experience over structured training programs.

How to Implement:
- Offer Leadership Development with Flexibility – Instead of lengthy workshops, provide short, actionable leadership training sessions.
- Encourage Skill-Based Promotions – Allow competency and contributions to dictate career progression, rather than time-based promotions.
- Create Cross-Functional Leadership Roles – Gen X thrives in dynamic, multi-departmental roles that allow them to apply diverse skills.

4. Engage Through Work-Life Balance and Flexibility

While Gen X values hard work, they were also the first generation to demand work-life balance. Unlike Boomers, who often sacrificed personal time for career advancement, Gen X leaders believe that professional success should not come at the cost of personal well-being.

How to Implement:

- Offer Hybrid and Flexible Work Options – Gen X managers are comfortable with remote work, provided that productivity remains high.
- Respect Boundaries – Encourage workplace policies that respect personal time, avoiding excessive after-hours communication.
- Provide Autonomy in Scheduling – Allow Gen X leaders to structure their workdays in a way that maximizes efficiency and personal productivity.

5. Foster Multi-Generational Collaboration

As the bridge generation, Gen X managers excel at balancing the perspectives of Boomers, Millennials, and Gen Z. They understand both traditional corporate structures and modern workplace dynamics, making them ideal mediators between generations.

How to Implement:

- Encourage Reverse Mentorship Programs – Pair Gen X leaders with younger employees to facilitate knowledge-sharing across age groups.

- Incorporate a Blend of Leadership Styles – Train Gen X managers to blend hierarchical and collaborative leadership models for multigenerational teams.
- Use Tech-Savvy Yet Practical Tools – Equip Gen X leaders with collaboration tools that balance traditional business processes with digital innovation (e.g., Slack, Asana, Zoom for remote teams).

6. Recognize and Retain Gen X Leaders

One of the biggest challenges companies face is retaining top Gen X talent, as many feel overlooked in favor of Boomers in leadership roles or Millennials being fast-tracked for promotions. Retaining Gen X leaders requires targeted incentives that align with their values.

How to Implement:
- Recognize Contribution Over Visibility – Many Gen X leaders prefer results-based recognition rather than public accolades.
- Offer Leadership Roles That Provide Influence, Not Just Title – Provide opportunities to lead strategic initiatives rather than simply promoting based on tenure.
- Ensure Compensation Reflects Value – Competitive pay, performance-based bonuses, and stock options resonate strongly with Gen X leaders who value financial security.

7. Modernize Without Alienating Them

While Gen X is adaptable, they don't embrace change just for the sake of it. They expect technological and structural changes to be practical and purposeful.

How to Implement:
- Adopt Change Gradually – Introduce new tools and policies incrementally, giving Gen X leaders time to adapt and provide input.
- Explain the "Why" Behind Changes – Avoid change fatigue by clearly communicating the business benefits of any transformation.
- Give Them a Role in Shaping the Future – Involve Gen X leaders in decision-making committees that influence workplace evolution.

Gen X leaders are practical, efficient, and highly independent, making them some of the most valuable assets in today's workforce. They thrive when they are trusted to lead without micromanagement, given meaningful career progression opportunities, and allowed to maintain work-life balance. Organizations that successfully integrate Gen X into leadership strategies will benefit from a no-nonsense, results-driven management style that strengthens team performance across all generations.

By implementing tailored leadership strategies, engagement techniques, and workplace policies, businesses can ensure that Gen X remains a driving force in shaping the future of leadership, bridging generational divides, and optimizing corporate efficiency.

But just as Gen X found itself navigating between Boomers and Millennials, Millennials have had to redefine leadership while dealing with expectations from both sides. As the first generation to prioritize work-life balance, purpose-driven careers, and technology integration, Millennials have challenged traditional corporate norms, often being labeled as "entitled" or "job-hoppers." Yet, their push for flexibility, innovation, and social impact has fundamentally reshaped the workplace. The question now is: how can businesses engage, motivate, and retain the largest working generation today?

Chapter 4: Millennials – The Purpose-Driven Employees

"We are not put on this earth to see through one another, but to see one another through."

— Gloria Vanderbilt

Q: "What does success look like to you?"

A: "Success is about doing work that matters. I don't want to just punch a clock and collect a paycheck—I want to feel like I'm contributing to something bigger than myself. Success isn't about staying at one company forever; it's about learning, growing, and finding purpose in what you do. If I can make a good living while also having time for my family, friends, and passions, then I've made it."

Chapter 4: Millennials – The Purpose-Driven Employees

Born between 1981 and 1996, Millennials have redefined the modern workplace with their emphasis on purpose, flexibility, and personal fulfillment. Unlike previous generations who viewed work primarily as a means to financial security, Millennials expect more from their careers—they want jobs that align with their values, offer opportunities for growth and impact, and provide a sense of meaning beyond just a paycheck.

Millennials entered the workforce during a period of rapid technological advancement, economic instability, and cultural shifts that shaped their professional expectations. Many witnessed the Great Recession, which disrupted traditional career paths and made them skeptical of long-term corporate loyalty. Unlike Baby Boomers, who prioritized stability and hierarchy, or Gen X, who favored independence and pragmatism, Millennials seek collaborative, mission-driven work environments that allow them to contribute meaningfully to something larger than themselves.

However, this generational shift has not come without challenges. Millennials have been labeled as "job-hoppers" due to their tendency to change roles more frequently than their predecessors. While some interpret this as a lack of commitment, Millennials see it as a pursuit of career fulfillment and skill development. They are not afraid to leave an organization that doesn't align with their values, provide growth opportunities, or prioritize employee well-being.

As a result, businesses have had to rethink traditional employment models to retain and engage Millennials effectively. Workplace culture, leadership styles, and employee benefits have evolved significantly due to Millennial expectations for work-life balance, mental health awareness, and career progression. Organizations that fail to adapt to these changing priorities risk high turnover, disengagement, and difficulty attracting top Millennial talent.

Despite some misconceptions, Millennials are highly motivated, innovative, and adaptable employees when placed in the right work environment. They thrive in collaborative, inclusive, and flexible workplaces where they feel valued, challenged, and aligned with the company's mission. Unlike previous generations, who were willing to compartmentalize their personal and professional identities, Millennials seek integration between work and life, preferring careers that reflect their personal passions and aspirations.

This chapter will explore what drives Millennials in the workplace, their emphasis on work-life balance and mission-driven work, and their tendency to job-hop in pursuit of fulfillment. We will also examine how businesses can keep them engaged without leading to burnout and provide practical tools for retaining and developing Millennials in leadership roles. By understanding what makes this generation tick, organizations can harness their energy, creativity, and ambition to create workplaces that thrive in an era of purpose-driven employment.

Work-Life Balance, Mission-Driven Work, and Job-Hopping Tendencies

Millennials have often been characterized as the generation that refuses to settle—not just in their careers but in how they approach work-life balance and professional fulfillment. Unlike previous generations who viewed work as a separate and necessary part of life, Millennials seek to integrate personal well-being, career aspirations, and a sense of purpose into one cohesive experience. They believe that work should align with their values, contribute to the greater good, and allow them the flexibility to enjoy life beyond office walls.

Redefining Work-Life Balance

For Baby Boomers, work was about paying dues and climbing the corporate ladder, while Gen X championed independence and career stability. Millennials, however, prioritize a work environment that allows them to live well while working hard. Work-life balance is not just a perk—it's an expectation. This shift is due to several key factors:

- Digital Connectivity: Millennials grew up with instant access to information and communication, meaning they are less tied to the traditional 9-to-5 schedule. They expect flexibility in when and where they work.

- **Mental Health Awareness:** Unlike previous generations, Millennials are more open about mental health challenges and advocate for workplaces that support emotional well-being.
- **Personal Fulfillment:** They don't see work as a separate part of life but as an extension of their identity and personal values. They want to feel energized by their work, not drained by it.

How Millennials Approach Work-Life Balance:
- They seek remote or hybrid work options that allow them to be productive without sacrificing personal time.
- They value paid time off (PTO) policies that encourage rest and travel.
- They prioritize health benefits and wellness initiatives that support their physical and mental well-being.
- They embrace side hustles and passion projects, seeing them as a way to explore creativity and additional income streams.

The Rise of Mission-Driven Work

A defining trait of Millennials is their desire to do meaningful work. They are not satisfied with jobs that simply offer a paycheck—they want to feel like their contributions make a difference. This has led to a rise in mission-driven work, where employees seek out companies that align with their values and social priorities.

What Mission-Driven Work Means to Millennials:

- Purpose Over Profit: Millennials are drawn to companies that have a strong corporate mission, whether it's environmental sustainability, diversity and inclusion, or social responsibility.
- Company Culture Matters: Beyond the mission statement, Millennials look at how a company treats its employees, whether it supports charitable initiatives, and whether leadership practices align with company values.
- Personal Growth and Development: They are not interested in stagnant roles. Millennials look for companies that provide growth opportunities, mentorship programs, and continuous learning initiatives.

Industries Thriving with Mission-Driven Millennials:

- Nonprofits & Social Enterprises: Many Millennials are drawn to careers in education, public service, and sustainability.
- Tech & Innovation: Companies that focus on disruptive technology, green energy, and ethical AI attract purpose-driven employees.
- Startups & Entrepreneurial Ventures: Millennials are highly entrepreneurial and are drawn to smaller, dynamic companies where they can have a direct impact.

Job-Hopping: Reality or Misconception?

One of the most controversial traits of Millennials in the workplace is their tendency to job-hop. Unlike Boomers, who often stayed with the same company for decades, Millennials are more likely to switch jobs every 2-3 years. While some employers see this as a lack of loyalty, Millennials view it differently:

- They prioritize career progression over tenure. If they feel stagnant in a role, they will move on rather than wait for a promotion that may never come.
- They seek better pay and benefits. Millennials entered the workforce during economic downturns and stagnant wages, making them more willing to switch jobs for financial growth.
- They want to expand their skill sets. By working in different environments, Millennials gain new experiences, industry knowledge, and valuable professional networks.
- They value workplace culture. If a company does not provide work-life balance, career development, or ethical leadership, Millennials will not hesitate to leave.

How Employers Can Adapt to Millennial Job-Hopping

Rather than viewing job-hopping as a liability, employers should adjust their strategies to retain Millennials by offering what they value most:

1. Career Development Opportunities – Provide clear career paths, leadership training, and internal mobility programs to keep Millennials engaged.
2. Competitive Compensation & Benefits – Ensure salaries are market-competitive, and offer perks like student loan assistance, wellness programs, and professional development stipends.
3. Strong Company Culture & Leadership – Create an environment that fosters open communication, transparency, and employee recognition.
4. Flexible Work Arrangements – Millennials appreciate remote work options, flexible schedules, and a results-oriented approach to productivity.

Millennials have reshaped the workplace by demanding flexibility, purpose, and growth. Their emphasis on work-life balance, mission-driven work, and job mobility has forced companies to rethink traditional employment models. While some businesses struggle to retain Millennial employees, those that adapt to their expectations will find themselves with highly engaged, innovative, and motivated teams.

In the next section, we will explore how businesses can keep Millennials engaged without burnout, ensuring they remain productive, fulfilled, and loyal employees.

How to Keep Millennials Engaged Without Burnout

Millennials have reshaped the workplace with their demand for meaningful work, flexibility, and professional development. While they are highly engaged and motivated when working in an environment that aligns with their values, they are also at higher risk of burnout than previous generations. The constant push for productivity, combined with economic pressures, job insecurity, and an always-connected digital culture, has led to a workforce that is engaged but often exhausted.

To retain and maximize the potential of Millennial employees, organizations must develop engagement strategies that prioritize well-being, sustainable workloads, and career satisfaction. Below are practical approaches to keeping Millennials engaged without leading them to burnout.

1. Redefine Engagement: Quality Over Quantity

Traditionally, employee engagement was measured by time spent at work, attendance at meetings, and visible participation. However, Millennials reject the notion that being busy equals being productive. They value engagement that leads to meaningful impact, not just checking boxes.

How to Implement:

- Focus on outcomes, not hours – Allow Millennials to structure their work around projects and results rather than strict schedules.
- Encourage asynchronous collaboration – Use tools that allow employees to contribute without needing to be present in every meeting.
- Provide autonomy in task management – Let employees choose how they work best rather than enforcing rigid processes.

2. Support Work-Life Integration, Not Just Balance

Work-life balance suggests a clear division between personal and professional life, but Millennials see work as an extension of their personal growth and passions. Instead of forcing separation, companies should embrace work-life integration, where employees can blend their professional and personal priorities in a sustainable way.

How to Implement:

- Offer flexible work hours that allow employees to manage their own time.
- Encourage mental health days and self-care initiatives to prevent burnout.

- Provide opportunities for side projects or passion-driven work within the company.

3. Foster a Culture of Continuous Learning

Millennials value professional development and skill-building as much as job stability. If they feel stagnant, they are more likely to seek opportunities elsewhere. Investing in continuous learning helps keep them engaged and reduces career fatigue.

How to Implement:
- Offer tuition reimbursement or stipends for professional development courses.
- Provide mentorship programs that connect Millennials with experienced leaders.
- Allow for cross-functional training so employees can explore different roles within the company.

4. Prioritize Employee Recognition and Appreciation

Millennials want to know that their work is valued and meaningful. While financial incentives are important, recognition can also come in the form of appreciation, opportunities, and trust.

How to Implement:

- Implement peer-to-peer recognition programs that allow employees to acknowledge each other's contributions.
- Encourage real-time feedback instead of waiting for annual performance reviews.
- Recognize employees with new challenges, leadership opportunities, or creative freedom to work on passion projects.

5. Encourage Authentic Leadership and Open Communication

Millennials appreciate authentic, transparent leadership that fosters open communication and trust. Leaders who share their challenges, mistakes, and successes resonate more with Millennial employees, creating a workplace where they feel valued and heard.

How to Implement:

- Hold regular town halls or Q&A sessions with leadership to encourage dialogue.
- Foster a coaching-based leadership style that prioritizes personal and professional growth.
- Promote psychological safety by encouraging employees to share ideas and feedback without fear of criticism.

6. Allow for Career Fluidity Without Stigma

Millennials do not view career progression as a straight line. Many prefer to explore different roles, industries, or skill sets over the course of their careers. Companies that offer internal mobility will retain more Millennial employees by preventing them from seeking growth opportunities elsewhere.

How to Implement:

- Create internal job rotation programs where employees can explore different departments.
- Support entrepreneurial initiatives within the company, such as innovation hubs or project-based work.
- Encourage employees to pivot within the company rather than leave when seeking change.

7. Promote Digital Wellness and Healthy Work Habits

Millennials are the first generation to experience 24/7 digital connectivity, leading to an "always-on" culture that contributes to burnout. Businesses must set boundaries to promote a healthy relationship with technology.

How to Implement:

- Establish "no email after hours" policies to prevent work from bleeding into personal time.

- Provide mental health resources and stress management workshops.
- Encourage employees to take vacations without guilt by modeling the behavior at leadership levels.

8. Build a Purpose-Driven Culture

Millennials engage most with companies that align with their personal values and social impact goals. Businesses that foster a purpose-driven culture will retain employees who feel emotionally connected to their work.

How to Implement:
- Develop corporate social responsibility (CSR) initiatives that involve employees in community service and social impact projects.
- Ensure company values are clearly defined and consistently upheld.
- Give employees a voice in shaping the company's direction and mission.

Millennials are one of the most engaged and purpose-driven generations in the workforce, but they are also at high risk of burnout if engagement strategies fail to account for their well-being. By fostering work-life integration, prioritizing continuous learning, recognizing achievements, and promoting digital wellness, businesses can sustain Millennial engagement without pushing them to exhaustion.

In the next section, we will explore practical tools for retaining and developing Millennials in leadership roles, ensuring they continue to grow and contribute meaningfully to the workforce.

Practical Tools: Best Ways to Retain and Develop Millennials in Leadership Roles

Millennials are stepping into leadership roles at an increasing rate, bringing new perspectives, digital fluency, and a strong desire for purpose-driven work. However, retaining and developing them into long-term leaders requires businesses to adapt traditional leadership development strategies to align with Millennial values. Unlike previous generations, Millennials do not see leadership as simply a title or a paycheck—they view it as an opportunity to make an impact, drive innovation, and build inclusive workplaces.

Organizations that successfully retain Millennials in leadership roles prioritize mentorship, career growth, flexibility, and continuous learning. Below are practical tools and strategies for developing and keeping Millennials engaged in leadership positions.

1. Redefine Leadership Development for the Millennial Mindset

Millennials do not respond well to rigid, top-down leadership training programs. They prefer personalized, hands-on development opportunities that allow them to grow through experience.

How to Implement:

- Offer Leadership Incubators – Create internal leadership accelerators where Millennials can take on strategic projects before formally stepping into leadership roles.
- Encourage Experiential Learning – Let Millennials learn leadership by leading real initiatives, rather than sitting in classrooms or attending seminars.
- Use Reverse Mentorship – Pair Millennial leaders with seasoned executives so that both parties can exchange knowledge and perspectives.

2. Provide Clear Career Pathways

Millennials are highly ambitious, but they dislike uncertainty in career progression. A lack of clear development paths often leads to job-hopping in search of better opportunities.

How to Implement:

- Define Transparent Career Tracks – Outline clear leadership pathways that Millennials can follow, complete with benchmarks for advancement.
- Offer Cross-Departmental Mobility – Encourage Millennials to explore different areas of the business before settling into leadership, allowing them to build a diverse skill set.

- Provide Regular Career Coaching – Assign career mentors or leadership coaches to Millennials, helping them navigate their professional growth.

3. Foster a Culture of Continuous Learning

Millennials value lifelong learning and seek leadership roles that challenge them intellectually. Businesses that invest in continuous education will retain top Millennial talent.

How to Implement:
- Sponsor Executive Education & Certifications – Provide stipends for leadership courses, executive MBAs, and industry certifications.
- Encourage Learning Sabbaticals – Offer paid leave for educational pursuits such as fellowships, specialized training, or leadership retreats.
- Create In-House Learning Labs – Develop digital and in-person learning hubs where Millennials can access leadership resources, training modules, and peer learning experiences.

4. Build Flexible Work Models for Leadership Roles

Unlike previous generations, Millennials do not see leadership as requiring constant presence in an office. They thrive in remote, hybrid, and flexible work environments.

How to Implement:

- Implement Hybrid Leadership Models – Allow Millennial leaders to manage teams remotely, providing tools and resources for virtual leadership.
- Focus on Output, Not Office Presence – Evaluate leadership success based on impact, innovation, and team performance rather than in-person attendance.
- Offer Leadership Roles with Work-Life Balance – Encourage Millennials to take mental health days, flexible vacations, and wellness breaks without stigma.

5. Develop Inclusive Leadership Training

Millennials value diversity, equity, and inclusion (DEI) in leadership. They expect businesses to prioritize inclusive leadership development that reflects a diverse workforce.

How to Implement:

- Integrate DEI into Leadership Training – Teach Millennial leaders how to foster diverse, inclusive workplaces.

- Promote Equal Access to Leadership – Ensure that leadership development programs are accessible to employees from all backgrounds.
- Encourage Diverse Leadership Teams – Create multi-generational and multi-cultural leadership groups to drive innovation and inclusivity.

6. Provide Purpose-Driven Leadership Opportunities

For Millennials, leadership is not just about authority—it's about making an impact. They thrive in leadership roles that allow them to drive social change, innovation, and meaningful transformation.

How to Implement:
- Give Millennials Ownership of Purpose-Driven Projects – Allow them to lead corporate social responsibility (CSR) initiatives.
- Encourage Mission-Driven Leadership – Align leadership roles with corporate missions that emphasize sustainability, ethics, and community impact.
- Incentivize Innovation – Reward Millennial leaders for proposing and implementing positive workplace and industry changes.

7. Prioritize Mental Health & Leadership Resilience

Millennials are more likely to burn out in leadership roles if they are not given the proper tools to balance responsibility with well-being.

How to Implement:

- Teach Stress Management for Leaders – Provide Millennial leaders with mental health resources, mindfulness training, and stress management coaching.
- Encourage Leadership Wellness Breaks – Offer leadership sabbaticals, mental health retreats, or flexible downtime.
- Create Support Networks for Millennial Leaders – Establish peer support groups where Millennial leaders can discuss challenges and share experiences.

8. Rethink Leadership Compensation & Incentives

Millennials are not solely motivated by money—they seek holistic compensation packages that include meaningful benefits, workplace flexibility, and recognition.

How to Implement:

- Offer Personalized Compensation Packages – Provide Millennials with customized benefits, such as student loan assistance, wellness stipends, and paid sabbaticals.

- Recognize Leadership Contributions in Non-Monetary Ways – Acknowledge Millennial leaders through career development opportunities, international projects, and industry recognition.
- Tie Compensation to Purpose & Impact – Reward Millennial leaders for achieving social impact goals, innovation milestones, and cultural contributions.

Millennials are redefining leadership by prioritizing flexibility, purpose, innovation, and inclusion. Businesses that adapt to their expectations will develop strong, motivated, and forward-thinking leaders. By offering personalized career growth, continuous learning, flexible leadership models, and purpose-driven leadership opportunities, organizations can retain Millennial talent and ensure long-term success in an evolving workforce.

But just as Millennials once disrupted the workplace with their emphasis on work-life balance and purpose-driven careers, Gen Z is taking things even further. This next generation isn't just shaping the future of work—they're demanding it be built on their terms. Born into a world of rapid technological advancements, instant communication, and limitless access to information, Gen Z approaches work with a digital-first mindset, bold expectations, and a demand for transparency like never before. As they enter the workforce in greater numbers, businesses must ask: How do we attract, engage, and retain a generation that expects workplaces to evolve as fast as they do?

Chapter 5: Gen Z – The Digital Disruptors

"The secret of change is to focus all of your energy, not on fighting the old, but on building the new."

— *Socrates*

Chapter 5: Gen Z – The Digital Disruptors

Q: "What does success look like to you?"

A: "Success is about freedom—freedom to work where I want, how I want, and on things that actually interest me. I don't see success as working my way up a corporate ladder—I see it as having control over my life. Whether that's through remote work, starting my own business, or having multiple income streams, I want to be able to make choices that align with my values. Success isn't just about money; it's about feeling mentally healthy, respected, and in charge of my future."

Born between 1997 and 2012, Generation Z is the first fully digital-native workforce, having grown up in an era of smartphones, social media, and instant access to information. Unlike Millennials, who witnessed the rise of digital technology as they entered adulthood, Gen Z has never known a world without high-speed internet, AI-powered tools, and algorithm-driven content. As a result, they bring a unique, fast-paced, and efficiency-driven approach to work that is already reshaping corporate culture.

Gen Z employees prioritize flexibility, fairness, and innovation, expecting businesses to adopt modern workplace practices that enhance productivity and foster inclusive, forward-thinking environments. While previous generations placed emphasis on job security, tenure, and hierarchical leadership, Gen Z is more entrepreneurial, adaptive, and purpose-driven. They seek workplaces that demonstrate fair hiring practices, equitable opportunities, and transparency in leadership, not just as corporate initiatives but as fundamental workplace values. If an employer lacks competitive flexibility, technological advancement, or a culture where employees feel valued, Gen Z has no hesitation in moving on to better opportunities.

However, this generational shift has led to tensions between Gen Z and older workers. Their direct, informal communication style, preference for texting over emails, and expectation for rapid feedback can sometimes frustrate Baby Boomers and Gen X managers accustomed to more traditional professional norms. Additionally, their demand for flexible work environments, mental health support, and leadership accountability can be misinterpreted as entitlement rather than a redefinition of workplace priorities.

Despite these differences, Gen Z is one of the most dynamic, resourceful, and tech-savvy generations to enter the workforce. Their collaborative mindset, adaptability, and digital fluency make them well-equipped to thrive in an era of automation, artificial intelligence, and digital transformation. Businesses that understand how to integrate Gen Z's expectations into company culture will benefit from their innovative thinking, problem-solving skills, and ability to navigate fast-changing industries.

This chapter will explore how Gen Z is redefining the workplace, why their communication style and work expectations can create challenges for older employees, and practical strategies for attracting, motivating, and retaining Gen Z talent. By understanding their mindset, organizations can embrace the strengths of this generation while fostering collaboration across all age groups.

Digital Natives Who Who Expect More Than Just Technology

Generation Z isn't just comfortable with technology—they've been shaped by it. From childhood, they've used apps, platforms, and AI tools to learn, communicate, shop, and socialize. Their worldview has been formed by instantaneous access, seamless interfaces, and intuitive design. That background doesn't just make them digitally fluent—it makes them deeply attuned to inefficiencies, especially in the workplace.

For Gen Z, outdated software, redundant meetings, or unnecessary red tape aren't minor annoyances—they're red flags. They expect work to move at the speed of their lives: automated, streamlined, and optimized. But they're not looking for flashy tools just for the sake of modernization—they're looking for technology that serves a purpose, enhances productivity, and respects their time.

This digital expectation also informs how they view leadership and organizational culture. Gen Z equates slow processes with resistance to change. If a company doesn't invest in user-friendly systems or fails to communicate efficiently across platforms, it signals more than inconvenience—it signals misalignment with Gen Z's values of innovation, clarity, and agility.

To retain top Gen Z talent, it's no longer enough to offer flexible work policies. Businesses must embrace intentional tech-forward practices that remove friction from workflows and allow younger employees to perform at their best. That means automating repetitive tasks, simplifying onboarding with digital tools, and embracing asynchronous communication without losing connection.

The companies that will thrive with Gen Z employees aren't just digital—they're digitally thoughtful. They pair innovation with accessibility, tools with training, and flexibility with accountability. And in doing so, they show Gen Z what leadership looks like in the modern workplace.

Flexibility: Work on Their Terms

One of the defining traits of Gen Z in the workplace is their demand for flexibility. While previous generations viewed remote work as a privilege, Gen Z sees it as a standard expectation. Having completed school, internships, and early career experiences in a time when remote and hybrid work became widely accepted, Gen Z employees expect location flexibility, adaptable schedules, and a results-driven work culture that focuses on productivity rather than rigid office hours.

What Flexibility Means to Gen Z:

- Remote and Hybrid Work Options: Unlike Boomers and Gen X, who built careers in office-centric environments, Gen Z prefers the freedom to work from anywhere while maintaining productivity.
- Asynchronous Work Models: Traditional 9-to-5 structures feel outdated to Gen Z, who favor output-driven performance over clocking in and out.
- Work-Life Balance as a Priority: Gen Z does not view work as their entire identity. They seek employers who respect personal time, offer wellness benefits, and encourage mental health awareness.
- Side Hustles and Entrepreneurial Interests: Many Gen Z professionals supplement their incomes with freelance work, content creation, or small business ventures, valuing financial independence and diverse revenue streams.

How Employers Can Adapt:

- Offer flexible scheduling that allows employees to work at their peak productivity hours rather than enforcing strict office times.
- Implement a Results-Only Work Environment (ROWE): Instead of focusing on where or when employees work, ROWE shifts the emphasis to outcomes and performance. Employees are held accountable for achieving key objectives

rather than logging a set number of hours, allowing for autonomy while ensuring business goals are met.

- Invest in remote collaboration tools such as Slack, Asana, and Notion to ensure seamless communication across teams, especially in hybrid or fully remote settings.
- Encourage autonomy and innovation: Recognize that side hustles and entrepreneurial interests don't mean disengagement. Businesses can tap into Gen Z's creativity by offering project-based leadership opportunities while supporting work-life balance through mental health days, no-meeting Fridays, and flexible PTO options.

A Modern Workplace: Fairness, Transparency, and Inclusive Leadership

Gen Z expects workplaces to reflect modern leadership practices that emphasize fairness, respect, and transparency. While previous generations may have viewed diversity and inclusion efforts as corporate initiatives, Gen Z expects these values to be naturally integrated into company culture. They want to work for employers who hire based on skills and potential, provide equal opportunities for career advancement, and foster an environment where different perspectives are welcomed.

What a Modern Workplace Means to Gen Z:

- Fair and Transparent Hiring Practices: Gen Z expects clear pay structures, bias-free interview processes, and equitable promotion opportunities.
- Inclusive and Open-Minded Leadership: They prefer leaders who listen to employees, encourage collaboration, and foster an environment where all voices are heard.
- Workplace Policies That Reflect Employee Needs: Instead of one-size-fits-all policies, Gen Z values individualized career development, mentorship programs, and leadership pipelines based on merit.
- A Culture of Psychological Safety: Employees should feel comfortable expressing ideas, taking risks, and challenging outdated workplace norms without fear of backlash.

How Employers Can Adapt:

- Go Beyond Lip Service: Gen Z is skeptical of performative inclusivity. Companies must show real policies and measurable progress in creating a workplace where employees feel valued.
- Offer Transparent Career Growth Paths: Provide structured career development plans, salary transparency, and leadership mentorship programs.
- Encourage Collaborative Decision-Making: Allow younger employees to have a say in company policies, innovation strategies, and workplace improvements.

- Promote Inclusive Leadership Training: Equip managers with tools to foster open communication, respect generational differences, and create adaptable leadership styles.

AI Integration: The Future of Work for Gen Z

Unlike older generations, who may see AI and automation as disruptive, Gen Z embraces AI as a productivity enhancer. From using AI-powered writing assistants to automating routine tasks, Gen Z expects businesses to leverage technology for efficiency and strategic decision-making.

What AI Integration Means to Gen Z:
- Automation of Repetitive Tasks: AI should handle mundane processes so employees can focus on creative and high-value work.
- AI as a Personal Productivity Tool: They use platforms like Notion AI, Grammarly, and ChatGPT to enhance workflow, writing, and decision-making.
- Digital Upskilling and AI Literacy: They expect employers to offer training in AI tools, automation software, and emerging digital trends.
- AI for Business Innovation: They want companies to use AI not just for efficiency but also for creativity, marketing, and problem-solving.

How Employers Can Adapt:

- Invest in AI Training & Digital Upskilling: Provide free courses on AI literacy, automation tools, and machine learning basics.
- Use AI Responsibly & Transparently: Ensure AI-driven decision-making tools prioritize fairness and accuracy.
- Encourage AI-Augmented Creativity: Foster a workplace where AI is seen as a tool to enhance human potential, not replace it.
- Equip Teams with AI-Powered Workflows: Implement tools that automate time-consuming administrative work, allowing employees to focus on strategic initiatives.

Gen Z is redefining the workplace by prioritizing flexibility, fairness, and AI-driven innovation. They are fast-moving, mission-driven, and highly adaptable, making them a valuable asset to organizations that embrace modern workplace principles. Companies that successfully integrate Gen Z's priorities—remote-friendly policies, leadership transparency, and AI-enhanced workflows—will be the ones that attract, engage, and retain the best of this generation.

In the next section, we will explore why Gen Z's communication style and work expectations can frustrate older workers—and how businesses can bridge these generational differences.

Why Their Communication Style and Work Expectations Can Frustrate Older Workers

One of the most noticeable generational shifts in the workplace today is the way Gen Z communicates and approaches work expectations. Their digital fluency, informal tone, and expectation for immediacy can often feel jarring to older generations who grew up in workplaces with more structured, hierarchical communication styles. While these differences can lead to friction, they also represent an opportunity for organizations to foster stronger, more adaptive teams by understanding how to bridge these gaps.

The Communication Divide

Unlike previous generations, Gen Z has been raised in an era of instant messaging, social media, and rapid-fire digital conversations. They are accustomed to quick responses, informal language, and emojis as part of professional discourse. While this style is efficient for them, it can feel unprofessional or even dismissive to Gen X and Baby Boomer colleagues, who value clear, structured, and often more formal communication.

1. Preference for Short, Direct Messaging

- Gen Z communicates through DMs, voice notes, and short emails. They often view long-winded emails or meetings as unnecessary and inefficient.
- Boomers and Gen X prefer structured, detailed responses. They often interpret short messages as lacking professionalism or respect.
- Potential Friction: A two-word Slack response ("Got it") from a Gen Z employee might come across as too informal or curt to a Gen X manager expecting a more detailed acknowledgment.

2. Use of Casual and Internet-Inspired Language

- Gen Z incorporates memes, GIFs, and emojis into communication, even in professional settings.
- Older generations may see this as unprofessional or lacking seriousness.
- Bridging the Gap: Organizations can establish communication guidelines that allow for casual, friendly interactions while maintaining professionalism in external-facing or formal correspondences.

3. Expectation for Instant Feedback

- Gen Z is used to real-time feedback loops from social media and gaming environments.

- They often expect quick responses from managers and may get frustrated with delayed email replies or drawn-out decision-making processes.
- Older generations, especially Boomers, are accustomed to weekly check-ins, formal performance reviews, and a more deliberate feedback cycle.
- How to Adapt: Managers can implement more frequent, bite-sized feedback sessions to satisfy Gen Z's need for constant learning and iteration while maintaining structured evaluations for long-term development.

Work Expectations: A New Way of Defining Productivity

Gen Z is redefining what it means to be productive, engaged, and committed to a workplace. Unlike Boomers, who measured productivity by hours logged, or Gen X, who prized independence and results, Gen Z emphasizes output, work-life integration, and purpose-driven work.

1. The Shift Away From the 9-to-5 Mentality
    - Gen Z views rigid work hours as outdated and believes in task-based productivity rather than time-based work.
    - Older generations often associate being physically present in the office with commitment and accountability.

- Potential Friction: A Gen Z employee finishing their tasks by 2 PM and logging off may be viewed as not working hard enough, even if they've completed their workload.
- Solution: Companies should shift toward results-driven performance metrics that focus on accomplishments rather than clocked hours.

2. Strong Demand for Work-Life Balance

- Unlike Gen X, who embraced work as a necessity, and Boomers, who valued loyalty to a company, Gen Z expects employers to prioritize mental health, well-being, and personal time.
- They see overworking as counterproductive and actively resist "hustle culture."
- Potential Friction: Older managers may interpret Gen Z's approach as lacking commitment rather than a shift toward healthier, long-term work habits.
- Bridging the Gap: Encourage conversations around wellness initiatives and realistic workload management to balance productivity with well-being.

3. Less Tolerance for Bureaucracy and Hierarchy

- Gen Z prefers flatter organizational structures where they can voice opinions, contribute ideas, and have direct access to leadership.

- Boomers and some Gen X leaders are used to earning influence through experience and tenure.
- Potential Friction: A Gen Z employee questioning a decision or challenging leadership in a meeting may be seen as disrespectful by a more traditional leader.
- Solution: Companies can create structured yet inclusive feedback loops that allow younger employees to share ideas while learning workplace norms about leadership dynamics.

Bridging the Gap Between Generations

Rather than viewing Gen Z's work habits as frustrating, organizations can implement strategies that balance the strengths of different generations and create a more cohesive, productive team.

1. Set Clear Communication Norms
   - Create company-wide guidelines for internal vs. external communication (e.g., formal email standards for external stakeholders, flexible Slack/DMs for team collaboration).
   - Encourage intergenerational mentorship, where Gen Z employees learn professional communication norms, and older workers adapt to more efficient digital tools.

2. Emphasize Results Over Presence
   - Adopt flexible work policies that focus on output and deadlines rather than hours worked.

- Develop hybrid meeting structures that allow teams to collaborate effectively without unnecessary office hours.

3. Implement Agile Feedback Systems
- Replace rigid annual performance reviews with more frequent micro-feedback loops.
- Train managers on how to provide constructive, real-time feedback in a way that motivates and engages Gen Z employees.

4. Create Inclusive Decision-Making Structures
- Encourage younger employees to contribute ideas while educating them on how decisions are made at an organizational level.
- Provide Gen Z employees with opportunities to lead small projects to help them understand business operations before stepping into larger leadership roles.

While Gen Z's communication style and work expectations may initially seem at odds with older generations, they represent a shift toward a more efficient, balanced, and technologically advanced workplace. By fostering mutual understanding, flexible policies, and open communication, organizations can bridge generational differences and leverage the strengths of all employees.

In the next section, we will explore practical strategies for attracting, motivating, and retaining Gen Z talent—ensuring that businesses stay competitive as the workforce continues to evolve.

Practical Tools: How to Attract, Motivate, and Retain Gen Z Employees

Attracting, motivating, and retaining Generation Z employees requires a shift in traditional workplace strategies. Unlike previous generations, Gen Z has grown up in an era of instant information, digital connectivity, and evolving workforce expectations. They value flexibility, purpose-driven work, continuous learning, and work-life balance—and they are unafraid to leave jobs that fail to meet their expectations. Companies that adapt to these needs will benefit from a workforce that Is tech-savvy, creative, and highly adaptable. Below are practical strategies for attracting, engaging, and keeping Gen Z employees committed to your organization.

1. Attracting Gen Z Employees: Creating a Workplace That Appeals to Them

A. Showcase Workplace Flexibility

Gen Z views flexibility as a non-negotiable rather than a perk. Unlike previous generations, who often equated long hours with dedication, Gen Z prioritizes results over hours worked and values the ability to structure their work around their personal productivity peaks.

How to Implement:
- Offer remote and hybrid work options to accommodate different work styles.
- Implement asynchronous work policies where employees can complete tasks at their most productive times.
- Use results-driven performance metrics instead of tracking time spent online or in the office.

B. Highlight Career Growth and Learning Opportunities

Gen Z employees want continuous development. They are more likely to stay with companies that offer clear career paths, skill-building programs, and mentorship opportunities.

How to Implement:
- Provide structured career roadmaps that outline potential growth opportunities within the company.
- Offer learning stipends, tuition reimbursement, and online course subscriptions.
- Pair Gen Z hires with mentorship programs where they can learn from experienced employees.

C. Demonstrate Your Company's Purpose and Values

Gen Z wants to work for companies that align with their values and contribute positively to society. They actively seek out employers that have clear corporate social responsibility (CSR) initiatives, environmental sustainability goals, and ethical business practices.

How to Implement:
- Clearly communicate your company's mission and values in job postings and recruitment materials.
- Highlight corporate initiatives that support social impact, sustainability, and ethical leadership.
- Offer paid volunteer days or programs where employees can contribute to causes they care about.

D. Leverage Social Media for Recruiting

Traditional job postings aren't enough to capture Gen Z's attention. They rely on social media, peer reviews, and company culture videos to assess potential employers.

How to Implement:
- Utilize LinkedIn, TikTok, and Instagram to showcase company culture and employee testimonials.
- Create short-form content that highlights what it's like to work at your organization.
- Encourage current employees to share their experiences on social media platforms.

2. Motivating Gen Z Employees: Keeping Them Engaged and Productive

A. Provide Frequent and Transparent Feedback

Unlike previous generations that were content with annual performance reviews, Gen Z thrives on continuous feedback and real-time recognition.

How to Implement:
- Implement biweekly or monthly check-ins to discuss progress and areas for growth.
- Use real-time performance tracking tools that allow employees to see their impact in real time.
- Encourage peer-to-peer recognition programs to foster a culture of appreciation.

B. Encourage Autonomy and Ownership

Gen Z prefers to take ownership of projects and make meaningful contributions rather than simply executing tasks.

How to Implement:
- Allow employees to take on leadership roles within projects early in their careers.
- Create cross-functional teams where they can collaborate with various departments.

- Encourage initiative by giving them the freedom to explore new ideas and propose solutions.

C. Support Mental Health and Well-Being

Mental health is a top priority for Gen Z employees, and they expect their workplaces to support wellness initiatives.

How to Implement:
- Provide comprehensive mental health benefits, including therapy stipends or on-site wellness programs.
- Normalize open conversations about mental health and encourage work-life balance.
- Offer wellness perks such as meditation apps, fitness reimbursements, or no-meeting days.

D. Foster a Collaborative and Inclusive Work Environment

Gen Z values inclusive workplaces where diverse perspectives are welcomed and team collaboration is encouraged.

How to Implement:
- Promote a culture of inclusivity by ensuring all employees have a voice in decision-making.
- Use collaboration tools like Slack, Miro, or Notion to streamline teamwork.
- Encourage open brainstorming sessions where employees at all levels can contribute ideas.

3. Retaining Gen Z Employees: Keeping Them Committed for the Long Term

A. Offer Personalized Career Growth Plans

Gen Z won't stay in a stagnant role for long. They need to see a clear future within the company.

How to Implement:

- Develop individualized career plans that align with employees' strengths and aspirations.
- Offer job rotation programs so employees can explore different departments and skill sets.
- Provide leadership development tracks for high-potential employees to move into management roles.

B. Create a Culture of Flexibility and Trust

Retention is higher in companies that treat employees as adults and trust them to get work done.

How to Implement:

- Allow employees to set their own schedules where possible.
- Avoid micromanagement—focus on outcomes, not hours worked.
- Provide options for compressed workweeks or additional PTO incentives.

C. Competitive Compensation and Benefits

While salary matters, Gen Z also values a well-rounded benefits package that supports overall well-being.

How to Implement:
- Offer student loan repayment assistance or tuition support.
- Provide generous PTO policies and mental health days.
- Ensure pay transparency to build trust and equity within the company.

D. Encourage Employee-Led Initiatives

Gen Z wants to feel empowered to contribute to workplace culture.

How to Implement:
- Support employee-led groups such as young professional networks, innovation task forces, or social impact teams.
- Encourage employees to pitch projects or new initiatives and provide funding or leadership support.
- Recognize contributions beyond traditional performance metrics, such as community involvement or mentorship efforts.

Attracting, motivating, and retaining Gen Z employees requires a modernized approach to workplace culture, leadership, and benefits.

By offering flexibility, career development, open communication, and purpose-driven work, businesses can cultivate loyal, engaged, and high-performing employees from this generation.

But just as companies are adapting to Gen Z's digital fluency and bold workplace expectations, an even younger generation is already waiting in the wings. Gen Alpha—those born into a world of AI, automation, and immersive technology—will enter the workforce with an entirely new perspective on what it means to work, learn, and lead. They won't just be digital natives; they'll be AI natives, expecting seamless integration of technology in all aspects of their careers. The question is no longer just how businesses adapt to younger generations—it's how they prepare a workforce shaped by technological acceleration, evolving education models, and entirely new ways of thinking about employment itself.

Chapter 6: Gen Alpha – The Future of Work

> *"The people who are crazy enough to think they can change the world are the ones who do."*
> — *Steve Jobs*

Q: "What does success look like to you?"

(Projected Response)

A: "Success is about creating something new and using technology to do things better. I don't want to follow someone else's path—I want to make my own. Whether that's designing something, starting a business, or working on projects I'm passionate about, success means being in control of what I do. I want to work smart, not just work hard. If I can make money doing something I actually enjoy, then that's success."

Generation Alpha, born from 2013 onward, represents the first fully AI-native generation—a cohort that will enter the workforce in a world defined by automation, augmented reality, and artificial intelligence. While Millennials adapted to digital transformation and Gen Z pushed for a technology-integrated workplace, Gen Alpha will likely blur the lines between human and machine collaboration in ways we've only begun to imagine.

This generation is growing up in an era where voice assistants, machine learning, and AI-generated content are everyday tools rather than novel innovations. Unlike previous generations that learned to use technology, Gen Alpha is learning through technology, engaging with personalized AI tutors, interactive digital experiences, and real-time global collaboration from a young age. Their familiarity with automation, algorithms, and data-driven decision-making will shape not only how they work but also what they expect from their employers and career paths.

At the same time, the rapid acceleration of AI-driven workflows, changing education systems, and an evolving global economy will mean that traditional career paths and workplace structures may look entirely different by the time Gen Alpha enters the job market. Concepts such as remote work, the gig economy, and digital-first business models will be second nature to them, and their approach to employment may challenge existing business structures even more than their Gen Z predecessors.

While we are still years away from seeing Gen Alpha as working professionals, business leaders and employers must anticipate the changes that this generation will bring. By understanding the key technological, social, and economic trends shaping their upbringing, businesses can begin preparing now for how to attract, engage, and integrate Gen Alpha employees in the workforce of the future.

This chapter will explore predictions on how Gen Alpha will shape the workforce, how AI and automation will redefine employment, and practical strategies business owners should implement today to prepare for this next generational shift.

Predictions on How Gen Alpha Will Shape the Workforce

As the first fully AI-native generation, Gen Alpha will enter a workforce that looks drastically different from today. With the rise of automation, machine learning, and global digital connectivity, they will likely redefine workplace norms in ways that challenge traditional business structures. Unlike previous generations that adapted to technology, Gen Alpha will be raised alongside AI as a collaborative tool, shaping their approach to work, communication, and innovation.

1. A Workforce Driven by Automation and AI Integration

By the time Gen Alpha enters the workforce, automation and AI-powered decision-making will be standard across industries. Routine tasks in fields like finance, healthcare, logistics, and even creative industries will be handled by intelligent systems, allowing employees to focus on higher-level strategy, problem-solving, and innovation.

How This Will Impact the Workforce:
- AI-Augmented Jobs: Instead of replacing jobs, AI will become a collaborative partner to Gen Alpha workers, enhancing efficiency and decision-making.

- Increased Demand for AI Literacy: Proficiency in AI tools, data analysis, and machine learning integration will be as fundamental as digital literacy is today.
- New Job Categories Will Emerge: Careers such as AI ethics consultants, human-machine interaction designers, and augmented reality specialists will be in high demand.

2. Hyper-Personalized Career Paths

Unlike previous generations who followed traditional career ladders, Gen Alpha will expect career experiences tailored to their personal skills and interests, largely shaped by data-driven career guidance and AI mentorship programs.

Key Shifts in Career Development:
- Dynamic Career Progression: Rather than climbing a single corporate ladder, Gen Alpha will likely follow fluid career paths, shifting between industries based on personalized skill-building and job-matching algorithms.
- Micro-Credentials and Continuous Learning: With AI-assisted learning, Gen Alpha may bypass traditional degrees in favor of specialized micro-certifications, skill-based credentialing, and real-time knowledge applications.
- Freelance and Project-Based Work Models: As automation reduces the need for full-time staffing in many roles, Gen

Alpha will thrive in a gig economy focused on project-based, high-value contributions.

3. A Fully Digital, Remote-First Workplace

With virtual collaboration tools, AI-driven workflows, and decentralized business models becoming the norm, Gen Alpha will expect flexible, remote-first workplaces that prioritize productivity over presence.

What This Means for Businesses:
- No More Physical Headquarters: Many companies will operate in virtual office environments, with remote work fully integrated into their business models.
- Borderless Talent Pools: Companies will be able to hire top talent from anywhere in the world, allowing Gen Alpha to work in truly global, cross-cultural teams.
- AI-Powered Productivity Tracking: Instead of clocking hours, businesses will focus on measurable output, creative problem-solving, and innovation as key performance indicators.

4. A New Era of Leadership and Workplace Culture

Gen Alpha will redefine leadership by embracing flat hierarchies, decentralized decision-making, and real-time collaboration. With exposure to AI-enhanced leadership training from an early age, they will bring a data-informed, emotionally intelligent approach to management.

The Future of Leadership:
- AI-Assisted Decision-Making: Leaders will use AI-driven insights to optimize business strategies, forecast trends, and personalize team management approaches.
- Emphasis on Emotional Intelligence (EQ): As automation handles technical tasks, human skills such as empathy, adaptability, and creativity will become leadership priorities.
- Values-Driven Workplaces: Gen Alpha will prioritize working for companies that align with their ethical beliefs, including sustainability, corporate transparency, and workplace inclusivity.

5. The Rise of Human-AI Collaboration

Rather than seeing AI as a tool, Gen Alpha will engage with AI as a co-worker, leveraging human-machine collaboration in nearly every industry.

Key Changes in Human-AI Interaction:
- AI-Powered Creativity: In fields like marketing, design, and content creation, AI will assist in brainstorming, prototyping,

and optimizing ideas, allowing human workers to focus on innovation and storytelling.
- Automated Routine Decision-Making: AI will handle time-consuming, repetitive decision-making tasks, freeing up Gen Alpha to work on high-level problem-solving and strategy.
- AI Mentors and Virtual Team Leaders: Instead of reporting to human managers, some Gen Alpha employees will receive real-time coaching, feedback, and career planning advice from AI-powered leadership systems.

6. A New Work Ethic: Meaning, Balance, and Purpose

With Gen Z already pushing for purpose-driven employment, work-life balance, and mental health awareness, Gen Alpha is likely to take these priorities even further.

The Future of Work Culture:
- Hyper-Customized Work Schedules: Employees will have AI-personalized schedules that optimize their work hours based on individual productivity cycles.
- Focus on Well-Being Over Work Hours: Mental health and workplace satisfaction will be prioritized, with businesses implementing AI-driven stress monitoring and well-being programs.

- Social Impact as a Career Requirement: Companies that fail to integrate ethical and social responsibility into their mission will struggle to attract Gen Alpha talent.

Gen Alpha is poised to transform the workforce by embracing automation, redefining career paths, and prioritizing human-AI collaboration. Unlike past generations, they will enter a highly personalized, remote-first, AI-enhanced job market where adaptability, creativity, and emotional intelligence are just as critical as technical skills.

As businesses prepare for the arrival of this next generation, leaders must start adapting workplace structures, redefining career development models, and embracing AI-powered management techniques to remain competitive in an era where human and machine collaboration is the new normal.

In the next section, we will explore how AI, automation, and new learning methods will redefine employment—and what companies need to do to prepare for these shifts now.

How AI, Automation, and New Learning Methods Will Redefine Employment

The rise of artificial intelligence, automation, and evolving learning methodologies is not just reshaping jobs—it is fundamentally altering how employment is structured, how skills are acquired, and how businesses operate. For Generation Alpha, these changes won't be disruptions; they will be the foundation of their professional world. Unlike previous generations who adapted to digital transformation, Gen Alpha will step into a workforce where AI is a collaborative partner, automation is an expectation, and continuous learning is a necessity.

As business leaders and educators look ahead, understanding these transformations is critical. Here, we explore how AI, automation, and innovative learning models will define the future of employment and what organizations must do to prepare.

1. AI as a Collaborative Workforce Partner

For decades, AI has been discussed as a tool for efficiency, but in the future workforce, it will function as a true collaborator rather than just an enhancer. This shift will fundamentally change the way jobs are structured and executed.

AI-Powered Collaboration in the Workplace:

- AI Co-Workers & Virtual Assistants: Employees will work alongside AI systems that handle data processing, administrative work, and predictive decision-making, allowing humans to focus on creative problem-solving and strategy.
- Real-Time AI Mentorship: AI-driven career coaching tools will provide personalized growth plans, feedback, and adaptive training, helping employees navigate career progression with AI as a mentor.
- Automated Project Management: AI will optimize workflows, delegate tasks based on skills, and provide real-time performance analytics, reducing inefficiencies and enhancing productivity.

What This Means for Businesses:

- Companies will need to train employees in AI literacy to ensure seamless human-AI collaboration.
- Businesses must invest in AI ethics frameworks to balance efficiency with responsible AI use.
- Leaders will need to redefine performance metrics, shifting from task completion to value-driven contributions.

2. The Automation of Routine Tasks & Workforce Adaptation

Automation is eliminating repetitive tasks across industries, but rather than replacing jobs outright, it is shifting the nature of human work toward higher-value activities. By the time Gen Alpha enters the workforce, automation will be deeply embedded in day-to-day operations across all sectors.

Industries Most Affected by Automation:
- Manufacturing & Logistics: Robotics and AI-driven inventory systems will reduce the need for manual labor but create new opportunities in robotic management and maintenance.
- Finance & Legal Services: AI-powered analytics will handle fraud detection, compliance auditing, and contract analysis, allowing professionals to focus on strategic decision-making.
- Healthcare: AI-assisted diagnostics, robotic surgeries, and predictive healthcare models will redefine patient care and medical research.

How Businesses Can Prepare:
- Redefine Job Roles: Companies should transition employees into strategic, supervisory, and creative positions as automation takes over routine work.

- **Upskill & Reskill Employees:** Businesses must offer continuous training programs to ensure employees are equipped with AI-driven skillsets.
- **Invest in Human-Centric Roles:** Despite automation, jobs requiring emotional intelligence, critical thinking, and human creativity will remain essential.

3. Personalized & AI-Driven Learning Will Replace Traditional Education Models

Formal education is shifting away from static, degree-based systems toward adaptive, personalized learning experiences powered by AI. For Gen Alpha, lifelong learning won't be an option—it will be the standard career expectation.

The Future of Learning & Skill Development:
- **AI-Powered Personalized Education:** Algorithms will tailor learning experiences to individuals, adapting to their progress and career goals in real time.
- **On-Demand Microlearning:** Employees will access bite-sized, job-specific training modules instead of spending years in formal education programs.
- **Immersive Learning Through VR & AR:** Augmented reality (AR) and virtual reality (VR) will create highly interactive, hands-on training experiences, eliminating the gap between education and practical application.

Implications for Employers & Educators:

- Degree Requirements Will Shift: Employers will move away from rigid degree-based hiring and instead prioritize skill-based certifications and AI-verified competencies.
- Continuous Learning Incentives: Businesses will provide employees with real-time skill development resources, ensuring ongoing adaptation to new technology.
- AI-Powered Training Programs: AI mentors will provide instant feedback and performance analytics, allowing employees to refine their skills dynamically.

4. The Gig Economy & Digital Nomadism Will Be the Norm

With increased automation and AI integration, the traditional concept of long-term employment will evolve. Gen Alpha will expect work to be flexible, project-based, and globally connected.

Key Workforce Trends:

- Task-Based Employment: Rather than committing to one employer, many professionals will work on a gig-based system, taking on multiple short-term, high-value projects.
- Decentralized & Remote Workplaces: Physical office spaces will be less relevant, as workforces become borderless and location-independent.

- AI-Powered Talent Matching: AI-driven platforms will match workers with customized job opportunities based on real-time skills assessments.

How Businesses Should Adapt:
- Develop Digital Work Ecosystems: Companies should invest in virtual offices, collaboration tools, and cloud-based infrastructures.
- Emphasize Project-Based Hiring Models: Businesses must transition from permanent roles to adaptive, contract-driven employment structures.
- Focus on Retention Through Flexibility: Offering customized career paths, work-life integration policies, and adaptive job roles will be crucial for keeping top talent.

5. Human Skills Will Become More Valuable Than Ever

With AI and automation handling repetitive tasks, human-centric skills—such as emotional intelligence, leadership, and creativity—will become the most sought-after professional attributes.

Critical Skills for the Future Workforce:
- Complex Problem-Solving & Critical Thinking: AI can analyze data, but humans will still be needed to interpret nuanced scenarios and make strategic decisions.

- Collaboration & Adaptability: Working seamlessly with AI-powered teams and cross-functional groups will be key to success.
- Emotional Intelligence & Ethical Decision-Making: As AI influences more aspects of business, human employees will need to ensure ethical responsibility and moral reasoning remain central to decision-making.

AI, automation, and personalized learning are not threats to employment but catalysts for transformation. For Gen Alpha, these technologies will be seamlessly integrated into their professional lives, shaping how they learn, work, and grow within organizations.

Businesses that embrace AI-powered collaboration, reimagine job roles, and prioritize continuous learning will be the ones that attract, engage, and retain the best talent in this new era of work.

In the next section, we will explore the practical steps business leaders need to take today to future-proof their organizations for Gen Alpha's workforce arrival.

Practical Tools: What Business Owners Need to Prepare for Now

With Generation Alpha set to enter the workforce in the coming decades, business owners must begin future-proofing their organizations today. While AI, automation, and evolving work models continue to shape the professional landscape, companies that proactively adapt will have a competitive advantage in attracting and retaining the best talent from this emerging generation.

Below are practical tools and strategies that business owners should implement now to ensure they are prepared for the future workforce that Gen Alpha will bring.

1. Implement AI-Driven Workflows and Digital Transformation

To stay relevant in the future workforce, businesses need to embrace AI and automation as fundamental components of operations. Companies that resist AI-driven processes will struggle to remain competitive as Gen Alpha employees expect workplaces that seamlessly integrate technology.

How to Implement:

- Adopt AI-Powered Productivity Tools – Use AI-driven software for data analysis, project management, and customer engagement.
- Invest in Automation – Automate repetitive, time-consuming tasks in areas such as finance, HR, customer service, and supply chain management.
- Provide AI Training for Employees – Offer AI literacy programs to current employees so they can integrate AI into their workflows before Gen Alpha arrives.
- Use AI for Talent Acquisition – Implement AI-driven recruitment tools that match candidates based on skills, behavioral analytics, and cultural fit.

By integrating AI into business functions now, organizations will create an environment where AI-human collaboration feels natural, making it easier to attract Gen Alpha talent in the future.

2. Create a Future-Ready Learning Culture

Gen Alpha will enter the workforce expecting continuous skill development. Traditional degrees will become less relevant, and skill-based hiring will take precedence over formal education.

How to Implement:

- Shift to Skill-Based Hiring – Rather than focusing solely on degrees, create hiring criteria based on competencies and experience.
- Invest in Microlearning Platforms – Use AI-driven learning tools like LinkedIn Learning, Coursera, and Udemy to provide continuous skill development.
- Offer Personalized Learning Paths – Implement adaptive learning platforms that tailor courses based on employees' individual learning styles and career goals.
- Encourage Cross-Training & Internal Mobility – Allow employees to rotate through different roles and departments, enhancing their adaptability and preparing for a dynamic workforce.

By embedding a culture of continuous learning, businesses will remain agile and attractive to Gen Alpha workers who will expect constant skill evolution.

3. Redefine Workplace Flexibility and Employee Expectations

Gen Alpha will expect flexibility to be a standard feature of employment, not a perk. Businesses must start adapting their work models now to prepare for a generation that will prioritize work-life integration over rigid schedules.

How to Implement:

- Develop Hybrid and Remote Work Models – Create policies that allow employees to work from anywhere while maintaining productivity.
- Implement Asynchronous Workflows – Move away from rigid schedules and allow employees to complete tasks based on their most productive hours.
- Focus on Outcome-Based Performance Metrics – Shift from tracking hours worked to measuring results and contributions.
- Invest in Digital Collaboration Tools – Adopt platforms like Slack, Zoom, Notion, and AI-driven productivity assistants to ensure seamless remote teamwork.

A flexible, remote-friendly, and results-driven workplace will make companies more attractive to Gen Alpha employees while improving efficiency for current workers.

4. Prioritize Ethical AI and Human-Centric Leadership

As AI becomes more embedded in daily work, business owners must balance technological efficiency with ethical considerations and human leadership.

How to Implement:

- Develop AI Governance Policies – Create guidelines to ensure that AI decisions are ethical, unbiased, and transparent.
- Train Leaders in Emotional Intelligence (EQ) – Future managers will need strong EQ skills to manage AI-assisted teams effectively.
- Balance AI and Human Decision-Making – Ensure that critical decisions retain human oversight, even when AI-driven insights are available.
- Create Transparent AI Policies for Employees – Educate teams on how AI is being used in decision-making processes and provide ways to challenge AI-based recommendations if necessary.

By proactively integrating ethical AI governance and human leadership principles, companies can prepare for a workforce where human-AI collaboration is the norm.

5. Build a Values-Driven Workplace Culture

Gen Alpha will seek purpose-driven employment, much like Gen Z, but with an even stronger expectation for corporate social responsibility (CSR), sustainability, and inclusivity.

How to Implement:

- Embed Sustainability into Business Practices – Reduce environmental impact by adopting green technologies, optimizing supply chains, and minimizing waste.
- Ensure Pay Transparency and Fair Hiring Practices – Promote equity and fairness in salary structures and hiring policies.
- Encourage Employee-Led Initiatives – Allow employees to propose and lead social impact projects that align with company goals.
- Integrate DEI Strategies in Everyday Work – Move beyond token initiatives and foster a truly inclusive culture where diverse perspectives are valued.

A company that actively supports social impact initiatives will be more appealing to future Gen Alpha talent, ensuring long-term retention and loyalty.

6. Prepare for a Gig-Based, Agile Workforce

The traditional full-time employment model is rapidly evolving. Gen Alpha will likely embrace freelance, contract, and project-based work, making agility a necessity for employers.

How to Implement:

- Develop Agile Hiring Models – Create a workforce strategy that includes full-time employees, contractors, and freelancers, allowing for more adaptability.
- Adopt AI-Powered Talent Matching – Use AI to match highly skilled professionals with project-based needs in real time.
- Offer Short-Term Work Opportunities – Develop internship and micro-apprenticeship programs that align with Gen Alpha's preference for hands-on experience.
- Focus on Retention Through Flexibility – Provide customized career paths, self-directed work opportunities, and flexible employment contracts to accommodate evolving job expectations.

By embracing a mix of full-time, contract, and freelance talent, businesses can stay competitive while appealing to Gen Alpha's preference for flexible, project-based work.

—

Business owners must begin preparing now for the workforce changes that Gen Alpha will bring. By integrating AI-driven processes, fostering a culture of continuous learning, embracing flexible work models, and prioritizing ethical leadership, companies can future-proof their organizations and stay ahead in an evolving job market.

Gen Alpha's expectations will be shaped by technology, adaptability, and purpose-driven work. Companies that proactively invest in AI integration, flexible employment structures, and values-based leadership will be best positioned to thrive in the workplace of tomorrow.

But thriving in the future of work isn't just about preparing for what's next—it's about managing the workforce that exists today. With five generations currently in the workforce, businesses must navigate a complex landscape of varying expectations, communication styles, and leadership approaches. The key to success isn't just understanding generational differences—it's knowing how to manage them effectively to foster collaboration, productivity, and long-term growth.

As we move into the last sections of this book, one thing is clear: the future of work is not just about adapting—it's about leading the change by creating workplaces where every generation works together seamlessly.

Chapter 7: Managing a Multigenerational Workforce

In today's workplace, it is not uncommon to find employees from four or even five different generations working side by side. From Silent Generation leaders still serving in advisory roles to Gen Z employees who expect digital fluency in every aspect of work, managing a multigenerational workforce presents unique challenges and opportunities. The diversity of perspectives, skills, and work preferences across generations can drive innovation, creativity, and productivity—but only if managed effectively.

Business owners and leaders must navigate differences in communication styles, workplace expectations, and technology adaptability to create an environment where every generation thrives. While generational gaps can sometimes lead to misunderstandings, frustration, or even workplace conflicts, the key to success lies in understanding what drives each generation and fostering collaboration rather than division.

Each generation brings valuable strengths to the workforce. Baby Boomers offer institutional knowledge and long-term perspective, Gen X contributes independent problem-solving and resilience, Millennials drive purpose-driven work and technological fluency, and Gen Z introduces fresh ideas and digital agility. Balancing these generational strengths while mitigating friction points is essential for business success in today's rapidly evolving workplace.

As leaders, the challenge is not just about accommodating generational differences but about leveraging them for business growth. How can organizations foster an inclusive and collaborative environment that benefits from multigenerational insights? How can managers ensure that team dynamics remain strong despite differing expectations and work styles? And what practical tools can businesses implement to make generational collaboration seamless and productive?

This chapter will explore how to prevent generational conflicts, the best leadership and communication strategies for each group, and practical tools like generational communication cheat sheets and team-building strategies. By understanding these dynamics, leaders can transform generational diversity from a potential challenge into one of their greatest business assets.

How to Prevent Generational Conflicts in the Workplace

A multigenerational workforce can be an organization's greatest asset—if managed correctly. However, differences in work habits, communication styles, and professional values can lead to misunderstandings and friction between employees of different age groups. Without the right strategies in place, generational conflicts can undermine productivity, morale, and teamwork. To create a thriving, collaborative work environment, business leaders must be proactive in identifying potential sources of conflict, addressing misunderstandings early, and fostering a culture of mutual respect.

Below, we explore common causes of generational conflict and practical strategies to prevent and resolve these tensions before they disrupt the workplace.

1. Recognizing the Root Causes of Generational Conflict

Before tackling generational conflicts, it's essential to understand where they stem from. Common causes include:

A. Differences in Communication Styles

- Older generations (Baby Boomers & Gen X) often prefer structured communication, such as formal emails or in-person meetings.
- Younger generations (Millennials & Gen Z) are more comfortable with short-form, digital communication, like instant messaging and video calls.
- Potential Conflict: Baby Boomers may perceive Millennials' brief emails as unprofessional, while Millennials may feel frustrated by lengthy meetings that could have been emails.

B. Contrasting Work Ethic & Expectations

- Baby Boomers value loyalty, long hours, and a strong work ethic.
- Gen X champions independence and self-sufficiency.
- Millennials and Gen Z prioritize work-life balance, mental well-being, and efficiency over time spent in the office.
- Potential Conflict: Older employees may see younger generations as "entitled" or "lacking work ethic," while younger employees may view traditionalists as resistant to change.

C. Differing Views on Hierarchy and Leadership

- Boomers & Gen X grew up in hierarchical corporate structures, respecting seniority and chain of command.

- Millennials & Gen Z favor flat hierarchies, where ideas matter more than titles, and collaboration is prioritized.
- Potential Conflict: A younger employee may challenge a senior manager's decision, thinking they are being proactive, while the manager may see this as disrespectful or insubordinate.

D. Varied Attitudes Toward Technology
- Boomers & some Gen Xers had to adapt to digital transformation and may struggle with new technologies.
- Millennials & Gen Z are digital natives, expecting fast adoption of AI, automation, and remote work tools.
- Potential Conflict: Older employees may resist new tech solutions, leading to frustration among younger colleagues who expect seamless digital integration.

2. Strategies to Prevent Generational Conflicts

Recognizing generational differences is only the first step—leaders must take deliberate action to prevent and manage conflicts. Below are key strategies to ensure a harmonious and productive work environment.

A. Foster an Open Dialogue and Mutual Understanding
One of the biggest sources of conflict is assumption and misinterpretation. Encouraging open conversations about work

preferences, communication styles, and expectations can create a foundation of understanding and respect.

How to Implement:
- Hold intergenerational workshops or discussion panels to allow employees to share insights into their work styles.
- Encourage storytelling—have employees discuss their career experiences and how the workplace has evolved.
- Create mentorship pairings where younger employees can teach digital skills to older workers while learning industry wisdom in return.

B. Offer Flexible Work Arrangements That Cater to All Generations

Workplace flexibility can reduce resentment and burnout across all age groups. Different generations have different lifestyle priorities, and accommodating these preferences can lead to increased job satisfaction and productivity.

How to Implement:
- Offer hybrid work options for employees who prefer remote work, while still providing office spaces for those who thrive in an in-person environment.
- Allow flexible schedules to support employees who prefer early or late work hours.

- Implement results-oriented performance tracking rather than measuring productivity solely by hours worked.

C. Adapt Communication Styles for a Multigenerational Audience

Since communication breakdowns are a primary cause of workplace conflict, adapting communication strategies can bridge generational gaps.

How to Implement:
- Use a mix of communication methods—emails for formal documentation, instant messaging for quick updates, and in-person/Zoom meetings for more in-depth discussions.
- Clarify expectations by ensuring that all employees understand when to use different communication channels.
- Encourage respectful and active listening across generations, ensuring everyone's voice is heard.

D. Redefine Leadership Approaches to Be Inclusive

Traditional, top-down leadership no longer works for all employees. A successful multigenerational workplace requires a leadership style that adapts to different motivational drivers.

How to Implement:

- Use situational leadership—adjust management approaches based on individual needs rather than a one-size-fits-all approach.
- Recognize and reward contributions in different ways—some employees appreciate public recognition, while others prefer private praise or tangible benefits.
- Encourage collaborative decision-making so employees of all generations feel valued and involved.

E. Promote Cross-Generational Teamwork

Fostering collaboration between different generations helps employees learn from each other's strengths rather than focus on their differences.

How to Implement:

- Create multigenerational project teams that bring together employees with complementary skill sets.
- Encourage knowledge-sharing by implementing job-shadowing programs.
- Use reverse mentorship programs where younger employees teach digital literacy while older employees provide career wisdom.

F. Establish Conflict Resolution Mechanisms

Despite best efforts, conflicts may still arise. Having a structured, fair resolution process ensures that issues are handled effectively before they escalate.

How to Implement:
- Train managers in conflict resolution skills tailored to generational dynamics.
- Encourage employees to voice concerns openly through confidential feedback channels.
- Use mediation when necessary to facilitate understanding and compromise.

3. The Business Benefits of Proactively Managing Generational Differences

A workplace that embraces generational diversity rather than allowing it to become a source of tension will reap numerous business benefits, including:

- Increased Innovation – Different perspectives foster creativity and fresh ideas.
- Stronger Team Performance – Employees who respect each other's work styles collaborate more effectively.
- Higher Retention Rates – When employees feel heard and valued, they are more likely to stay.

- Competitive Advantage – Companies that successfully integrate multiple generations will adapt better to market changes and emerging trends.

Preventing generational conflicts in the workplace requires proactive leadership, open communication, and a culture of mutual respect. Instead of seeing generational differences as barriers, companies that embrace collaboration, flexibility, and adaptive leadership will benefit from the unique strengths each generation brings.

In the next section, we will explore the best leadership and communication styles for managing a multigenerational workforce, ensuring that every employee—regardless of age—feels engaged, valued, and motivated.

The Best Leadership and Communication Styles for Each Group

Effectively managing a multigenerational workforce requires a leadership approach that adapts to different work styles, values, and expectations. Each generation brings unique strengths, challenges, and communication preferences, meaning that one-size-fits-all leadership simply doesn't work. Instead, business leaders must tailor their approach to motivate, engage, and communicate effectively with each group.

Below, we explore the best leadership and communication strategies for each generation, ensuring that every employee—regardless of age—feels valued, understood, and empowered to perform at their best.

1. Leadership and Communication Styles for the Silent Generation (Born 1928–1945)

The Silent Generation is largely retired, but some are still involved in the workforce as board members, consultants, or mentors. They bring deep institutional knowledge, discipline, and a traditional work ethic.

Best Leadership Approaches:
- Respect for hierarchy: This generation responds well to structured leadership with clear roles and expectations.
- Emphasis on legacy: Many in this generation want to pass down knowledge and leave a lasting impact on the organization.
- Stability and consistency: They prefer long-term strategies over rapid change.

Best Communication Strategies:
- Use formal, respectful language in interactions.
- Prefer face-to-face meetings or phone calls over digital communication.
- Appreciate recognition for their experience and wisdom.

How to Lead Them Effectively:
- Assign mentorship roles where they can pass down expertise to younger generations.
- Acknowledge their contributions and institutional knowledge.
- Provide structured and well-documented communication.

2. Leadership and Communication Styles for Baby Boomers (Born 1946–1964)

Boomers are known for their strong work ethic, loyalty, and preference for structured corporate environments. Many have leadership roles or serve as senior advisors.

Best Leadership Approaches:
- Authoritative yet collaborative: They respect hierarchy but appreciate when leaders value their input.
- Recognition-driven: They respond well to public recognition of their experience and hard work.
- Commitment to professionalism: They prefer clear roles, responsibilities, and stability.

Best Communication Strategies:
- Use direct, professional, and detailed communication.
- Prefer emails, phone calls, or scheduled meetings over instant messaging.
- Appreciate formal recognition, awards, or appreciation in front of peers.

How to Lead Them Effectively:
- Involve them in strategic decision-making so they feel valued.
- Provide opportunities for mentorship and leadership training.

- Respect their traditional approach to work, but introduce new methods gradually.

3. Leadership and Communication Styles for Generation X (Born 1965–1980)

Gen Xers are independent, self-reliant, and results-driven. They grew up in a time of economic shifts, making them adaptable and pragmatic.

Best Leadership Approaches:
- Autonomy and flexibility: Gen X thrives under leaders who give them space to work independently.
- Straightforward, no-nonsense leadership: They respect direct, honest feedback.
- Balanced work-life integration: They appreciate leaders who prioritize efficiency over long hours.

Best Communication Strategies:
- Prefer concise, results-oriented communication.
- Appreciate email or direct messaging over lengthy meetings.
- Value honest, constructive feedback without unnecessary formality.

How to Lead Them Effectively:
- Avoid micromanagement—trust them to complete their work.

- Provide opportunities for leadership roles without rigid corporate structures.
- Offer flexible work arrangements to maintain work-life balance.

4. Leadership and Communication Styles for Millennials (Born 1981–1996)

Millennials seek meaningful work, career growth, and flexibility. They value collaboration, transparency, and a sense of purpose in the workplace.

Best Leadership Approaches:
- Coaching and mentorship over traditional authority: Millennials prefer leaders who act as mentors rather than strict managers.
- Purpose-driven leadership: They want to work for companies that align with their personal values.
- Collaboration and teamwork: They excel in open, inclusive, and team-oriented work environments.

Best Communication Strategies:
- Prefer transparent, open, and ongoing feedback rather than formal reviews.
- Comfortable with instant messaging, video calls, and digital communication tools.

- Respond well to personalized praise and growth-oriented feedback.

How to Lead Them Effectively:
- Provide opportunities for learning, development, and career advancement.
- Encourage team collaboration and input on company decisions.
- Use technology to streamline communication and engagement.

5. Leadership and Communication Styles for Generation Z (Born 1997–2012)

Gen Z is the first fully digital-native workforce, valuing speed, adaptability, and inclusivity. They seek authenticity, digital communication, and career flexibility.

Best Leadership Approaches:
- Transparent and inclusive leadership: They value leaders who communicate openly and honestly.
- Encouragement of individuality and innovation: They want opportunities to express creativity.
- Diversity, inclusion, and fairness: They expect leadership to actively support social impact initiatives.

Best Communication Strategies:

- Prefer short-form, instant digital communication (Slack, WhatsApp, video calls).
- Respond well to interactive and visual communication (infographics, short videos, real-time feedback).
- Appreciate authentic, direct conversations over corporate jargon.

How to Lead Them Effectively:

- Use interactive and digital communication tools for engagement.
- Provide clear career development paths and mentorship opportunities.
- Foster an inclusive, purpose-driven company culture.

Leading a multigenerational workforce requires adaptability, empathy, and a willingness to adjust leadership and communication styles. The most effective leaders recognize that each generation brings valuable strengths—and by understanding their preferences, businesses can build more engaged, productive, and collaborative teams.

In the next section, we will explore practical tools, including a generational communication cheat sheet and team-building strategies, to help leaders foster stronger connections across age groups.

Practical Tools: Generational Communication Cheat Sheet and Team-Building Strategies

Managing a multigenerational workforce requires effective communication strategies and team-building approaches that cater to the diverse needs and preferences of each generation. A well-structured workplace fosters collaboration, inclusivity, and mutual respect, reducing misunderstandings and maximizing productivity.

This section provides a generational communication cheat sheet and team-building strategies that business leaders can implement to enhance teamwork and workplace harmony.

1. Generational Communication Cheat Sheet

Each generation has unique communication preferences, shaped by the technology and workplace culture of their formative years. This cheat sheet offers a quick guide to adjusting communication styles to improve collaboration and minimize friction across age groups.

Generation	Preferred Communication Style	Best Practices	What to Avoid
Silent Generation (1928–1945)	Formal, structured, face-to-face or phone calls	Use clear, respectful language; schedule meetings with set agendas	Overly casual tone, reliance on digital-only communication
Baby Boomers (1946–1964)	Direct, professional, detailed emails or calls	Acknowledge experience, use structured communication, provide in-person options	Short, vague messages, excessive use of slang or emojis
Generation X (1965–1980)	Concise, efficient, results-focused	Be direct, respect independence, offer flexibility	Micromanagement, excessive meetings, overly formal language
Millennials (1981–1996)	Collaborative, digital-first, transparent	Use Slack, Zoom, and instant messaging; provide real-time feedback	Rigid corporate hierarchy, slow response times, lack of transparency
Generation Z (1997–2012)	Short-form, fast-paced, visual, authentic	Incorporate video messages, interactive content, direct feedback	Bureaucratic language, long emails, excessive formalities

How to Use This Cheat Sheet

- Adapt communication styles to match generational preferences.
- Provide multiple communication channels to meet diverse needs.
- Encourage mutual understanding by explaining why different generations communicate the way they do.

2. Team-Building Strategies for a Multigenerational Workforce

Building a cohesive team across generations requires intentional strategies that promote collaboration, knowledge-sharing, and respect. Below are proven team-building methods to strengthen intergenerational relationships in the workplace.

A. Implement Reverse Mentorship Programs

One of the most effective ways to bridge generational gaps is through reverse mentorship, where younger employees mentor older colleagues on technology, social trends, and modern work practices, while older employees share industry knowledge and leadership insights.

How to Implement:
- Pair a younger employee with a senior employee for mutual learning.
- Focus on technology training, leadership skills, and cultural shifts.
- Set structured check-ins to ensure continuous engagement.

Why It Works:
- Encourages knowledge-sharing in both directions.
- Reduces generational biases and stereotypes.
- Strengthens cross-generational teamwork and trust.

B. Host Generational Collaboration Workshops

Workshops that explore each generation's strengths, work styles, and communication preferences can help employees understand and appreciate their colleagues' perspectives.

How to Implement:
- Facilitate open discussions on workplace preferences and challenges.
- Conduct team-building exercises that highlight generational strengths.
- Include role-playing activities to encourage empathy and understanding.

Why It Works:
- Reduces workplace misunderstandings by addressing stereotypes head-on.
- Encourages cross-generational appreciation and learning.
- Creates a culture of inclusivity and respect.

C. Create Cross-Generational Project Teams

Encourage employees from different generations to work together on high-impact projects, allowing them to leverage each other's skills and experiences.

How to Implement:
- Form teams with representatives from multiple generations.
- Assign tasks based on strengths rather than age.
- Promote collaborative problem-solving and innovation.

Why It Works:

- Leverages diverse skill sets for well-rounded decision-making.
- Improves team cohesion and knowledge transfer.
- Enhances creative thinking and problem-solving.

D. Encourage Social Connection Through Informal Gatherings

Social events and informal interactions help break down generational barriers and foster stronger working relationships.

How to Implement:

- Organize lunch-and-learns where employees share their expertise.
- Host multigenerational networking events.
- Encourage cross-departmental social activities.

Why It Works:

- Strengthens team relationships outside of work tasks.
- Encourages natural conversations and relationship-building.
- Reduces generational silos and workplace cliques.

E. Recognize and Celebrate Generational Contributions

Acknowledging the contributions of different generations fosters respect and appreciation.

How to Implement:

- Highlight employee milestones and achievements from each generation.
- Implement a recognition program that includes public appreciation.
- Encourage employees to nominate colleagues for their contributions.

Why It Works:

- Boosts morale and engagement across all generations.
- Reinforces a culture of mutual respect.
- Encourages collaborative, supportive work environments.

By leveraging tailored communication strategies and intentional team-building efforts, organizations can turn generational diversity into a powerful advantage. When businesses embrace adaptable leadership, open dialogue, and inclusive collaboration, they create workplaces where employees of all ages can thrive together.

As we wrap up this book, it's clear that managing a multigenerational workforce is not about eliminating differences—it's about learning how to use them as strengths. The companies that master generational collaboration won't just keep up with workplace evolution; they'll drive it. But what does that evolution actually look like? What's on the horizon for hiring, retention, and company culture as new trends, technologies, and workforce expectations take shape?

In our final chapter, we'll explore the biggest generational shifts coming in the next decade, how businesses can prepare for the unexpected, and the practical steps leaders can take today to build a future-ready workforce.

Chapter 8: WTF Happens Next?

The workplace is constantly evolving, and as we look to the future, business owners, leaders, and employees alike must prepare for a generational shift that will redefine hiring, retention, and company culture. Over the next decade, the workforce will see an even greater blend of Millennials in leadership roles, Gen Z maturing into mid-career professionals, and the emergence of Gen Alpha—a generation raised in a fully digital and AI-integrated world.

Understanding how these transitions will shape the workplace is not just important—it's critical for business survival. Hiring practices will become more data-driven and skill-focused, company cultures will need to be more adaptive and inclusive, and retention strategies will require businesses to think beyond traditional benefits and career paths. What worked for Baby Boomers and Gen X won't necessarily work for Millennials and Gen Z, and what engages Gen Z today may not hold Gen Alpha's attention tomorrow.

The challenge for business owners and leaders isn't just keeping up with these changes—it's anticipating and leading them. This requires a deep understanding of what motivates each generation, how to attract and retain top talent, and how to build a workplace culture that is resilient, forward-thinking, and adaptable to the shifting expectations of employees.

As we move into this next era of work, one thing is certain: organizations that fail to embrace generational evolution will struggle to stay competitive. The companies that thrive will be those that innovate their hiring practices, redefine leadership, and create work environments that support intergenerational collaboration.

This chapter will explore the future of hiring, retention, and company culture, the biggest generational shifts coming in the next decade, and provide a self-assessment tool for business owners to measure their generational awareness. By the end, you'll have the knowledge and tools to ensure your business is future-proofed and positioned for long-term success in an ever-changing workforce landscape.

The Future of Hiring, Retention, and Company Culture

As businesses prepare for the next wave of workforce evolution, hiring, retention, and company culture will undergo significant transformations. The traditional approach of filling roles based on rigid qualifications and lengthy tenure expectations is giving way to skill-based hiring, dynamic career paths, and purpose-driven workplace cultures. To remain competitive, organizations must rethink their strategies, adopting flexible, forward-thinking approaches that align with the expectations of Millennials, Gen Z, and the incoming Gen Alpha workforce.

1. The Future of Hiring: Moving Beyond Resumes

Hiring in the coming decade will be less about degrees and more about skills, adaptability, and cultural fit. Employers will rely heavily on AI-driven talent acquisition, automated assessments, and data-backed hiring decisions to ensure the best candidates are selected based on merit rather than traditional credentials.

Key Hiring Trends:
- Skill-Based Hiring Over Degree Requirements: Companies will prioritize technical skills, soft skills, and problem-solving abilities over formal education. Microcredentials,

apprenticeships, and real-world experience will become more valuable than traditional degrees.
- AI-Powered Talent Acquisition: AI-driven applicant tracking systems will help businesses analyze candidate skills, personality traits, and compatibility with company culture before the first interview even takes place.
- Gamification in Hiring Processes: Businesses will incorporate AI simulations, problem-solving tasks, and virtual reality assessments to gauge candidate abilities in real-world scenarios rather than relying on a resume and cover letter.
- Hiring for Adaptability: With the speed of technological change, businesses will seek employees who can learn new skills quickly, rather than those with static expertise.
- Diversity and Inclusion Will Be Data-Driven: AI will be used to identify unconscious biases in hiring practices, ensuring more diverse, inclusive hiring decisions that bring fresh perspectives into the workplace.

How to Adapt:
- Adopt skills-based hiring practices by focusing on competencies rather than rigid degree requirements.
- Leverage AI-driven recruitment tools to enhance efficiency and reduce hiring biases.
- Redesign job descriptions to emphasize adaptability, innovation, and mission alignment rather than just technical skills.

2. The Future of Retention: Keeping Employees Engaged and Invested

Once businesses hire the right talent, the next challenge is keeping them engaged, productive, and committed. The concept of "lifetime employment" is rapidly disappearing—Millennials and Gen Z employees are not afraid to job-hop if they feel undervalued or stagnant. Retention strategies must evolve to accommodate flexible career paths, personalized development plans, and a work environment that fosters purpose and well-being.

Key Retention Trends:
- Personalized Career Growth Plans: One-size-fits-all career ladders will become obsolete. Instead, businesses will offer individualized career paths, allowing employees to choose roles that align with their evolving skills and passions.
- On-Demand Learning & Upskilling: Companies will integrate AI-driven learning platforms that provide personalized training, enabling employees to acquire new skills without leaving their roles.
- Wellness and Mental Health Support: Businesses will recognize that employee well-being directly impacts productivity and retention. Flexible work schedules, mental health days, and wellness stipends will become standard.
- Employee Experience Over Traditional Perks: While ping-pong tables and free lunches were once selling points, future

employees will value transparent leadership, meaningful work, and a sense of belonging over flashy office perks.
- Performance Reviews Will Be Replaced by Real-Time Feedback: Employees will expect continuous coaching and feedback loops rather than once-a-year performance appraisals.

How to Adapt:
- Invest in continuous learning platforms that provide AI-driven, on-demand training for employees.
- Offer flexible career paths that allow employees to pivot into new roles and industries within the company.
- Create a well-being-centered culture with mental health support, personalized benefits, and flexible work options.
- Adopt real-time feedback tools that allow for frequent, constructive conversations between employees and managers.

3. The Future of Company Culture: Redefining What Work Means

The future of company culture is not about office layouts, corporate retreats, or dress codes—it's about creating an ecosystem that fosters engagement, inclusivity, and long-term purpose. Businesses that build authentic, mission-driven cultures will attract top talent and keep employees engaged, regardless of generational differences.

Key Company Culture Trends:

- Hybrid and Remote-First Work Environments: The concept of a physical office as the center of company culture will continue to fade. Businesses will shift toward virtual-first models, where employees engage in digital collaboration spaces while having the option for in-person experiences.
- Trust and Autonomy Over Micromanagement: Employees will expect trust-based cultures, where they are evaluated based on results rather than micromanaged by outdated attendance metrics.
- Authentic Leadership and Transparency: Employees—especially Millennials and Gen Z—will demand transparent leadership, where executives engage in open dialogue about company decisions, challenges, and long-term visions.
- Sustainability and Social Responsibility Will Be Non-Negotiable: Future employees will expect companies to demonstrate real action on issues like sustainability, equity, and ethical business practices.
- Cross-Generational Knowledge Sharing: To bridge the experience gap between older and younger employees, businesses will need to develop mentorship networks, knowledge-sharing initiatives, and leadership pipelines that leverage multigenerational strengths.

How to Adapt:

- Embrace hybrid work models that balance flexibility with in-person collaboration opportunities.
- Shift from micromanagement to trust-based leadership by empowering employees with autonomy.
- Prioritize social impact initiatives that align with employee values, demonstrating an authentic commitment to sustainability and ethics.
- Implement mentorship programs that foster multigenerational learning and knowledge transfer.

The future of hiring, retention, and company culture is about adaptability, inclusivity, and purpose-driven work environments. Businesses that successfully integrate AI-powered hiring, flexible career paths, well-being-centered retention strategies, and value-driven cultures will be the ones that attract and retain top talent in an ever-evolving workforce.

As we move forward, organizations must be willing to challenge outdated practices, embrace technological advancements, and prioritize human-centered leadership. The companies that lead this transformation won't just survive the generational shift—they will set the standard for the future of work.

In the next section, we will explore the biggest generational shifts coming in the next decade and what businesses must do now to prepare for these changes.

The Biggest Generational Shifts Coming in the Next Decade

As we look ahead, the workforce will experience unprecedented generational shifts that will redefine how businesses operate, communicate, and engage employees. With Baby Boomers retiring, Millennials taking over leadership roles, Gen Z advancing into mid-career positions, and Gen Alpha beginning to enter the workforce, organizations must prepare for an evolving landscape where expectations around work, technology, and culture will continue to shift.

Understanding these generational transitions will help businesses anticipate challenges, seize opportunities, and develop forward-thinking strategies to remain competitive. Here, we explore the most significant generational changes coming in the next decade and what they mean for business leaders.

1. The Final Transition of Baby Boomers from the Workforce

What's Changing?

- By 2030, all Baby Boomers will have reached retirement age, marking the largest exit of experienced professionals in history.

- Many industries, particularly those that rely on institutional knowledge and leadership experience, will feel the impact of this transition.
- The knowledge gap left behind will create an urgent need for mentorship programs, leadership pipelines, and knowledge transfer strategies.

What Businesses Must Do to Prepare:
- Establish Succession Planning Now – Ensure that critical knowledge and leadership expertise are passed down through mentorship and structured transition plans.
- Capture Institutional Knowledge Digitally – Use AI-powered documentation, video recordings, and digital knowledge bases to retain industry best practices.
- Encourage Flexible Retirement Models – Offer consulting roles or part-time advisory positions to leverage Baby Boomers' experience while transitioning leadership to younger generations.

2. Millennials Becoming the Dominant Leadership Group

What's Changing?
- Millennials, born between 1981 and 1996, will hold most leadership positions by 2030.

- Unlike previous generations, they prioritize collaborative decision-making, purpose-driven leadership, and flexibility.
- They will reshape corporate culture by emphasizing inclusivity, transparency, and work-life balance.

What Businesses Must Do to Prepare:
- Support Millennial Leadership Development – Provide executive coaching, leadership training, and mentorship opportunities.
- Shift to Flexible and Inclusive Management Styles – Adapt workplace policies to prioritize employee well-being, mental health, and remote work flexibility.
- Align Company Values with Millennial Priorities – Ensure that corporate social responsibility (CSR) and environmental sustainability are deeply embedded in company culture.

3. Gen Z's Influence on Workplace Norms

What's Changing?
- By 2035, Gen Z will make up nearly one-third of the global workforce, influencing workplace expectations and operational structures.
- They demand workplace authenticity, rapid career progression, and diversity in leadership.

- Their digital fluency and preference for non-traditional career paths will accelerate changes in recruitment and employee engagement.

What Businesses Must Do to Prepare:
- Enhance Digital Employee Experience – Invest in AI-driven tools, virtual collaboration platforms, and real-time performance feedback systems.
- Emphasize Skills-Based Career Growth – Provide non-linear career paths, project-based work, and AI-driven career planning.
- Prioritize Transparency and Ethical Leadership – Maintain open communication, fair pay policies, and genuine DEI (diversity, equity, inclusion) commitments.

4. The Arrival of Gen Alpha: The AI-Native Workforce

What's Changing?
- Gen Alpha, born after 2012, will enter the workforce by 2030, bringing with them a seamless integration of AI, automation, and digital collaboration.
- They will expect AI-enhanced workflows, highly customized career experiences, and gamified learning environments.
- Unlike previous generations, they will have no memory of a pre-digital workplace, meaning traditional corporate structures may feel outdated to them.

What Businesses Must Do to Prepare:
- Invest in AI-Powered Training and Development – Use personalized learning platforms, interactive VR training, and AI mentorship tools.
- Adapt to a Hyper-Flexible Work Model – Implement task-based, gig-style work structures with on-demand employment opportunities.
- Leverage Automation for Repetitive Tasks – Free up employees to focus on high-value, creative, and strategic work.

5. The Reinvention of the Traditional Career Path

What's Changing?
- The traditional career ladder will be replaced by career "lattices", allowing employees to move laterally, cross-functionally, and internationally within organizations.
- Companies will deprioritize tenure-based promotions and instead focus on skills development and project-based career growth.
- AI-driven career planning will allow employees to receive personalized job recommendations, training, and mentorship opportunities.

What Businesses Must Do to Prepare:

- Offer Continuous Learning & Upskilling – Implement real-time, AI-driven skills training to help employees advance based on performance, not tenure.
- Redefine Career Progression Metrics – Move away from time-based promotions to a system based on achievements, innovation, and leadership potential.
- Encourage Cross-Departmental Experience – Allow employees to explore multiple roles within the company, enhancing engagement and retention.

6. The Workplace Becomes a Hub for Social Impact

What's Changing?

- Employees across generations will expect their workplaces to lead on social issues, including sustainability, ethical AI use, and corporate transparency.
- "Purpose-driven work" will become a deciding factor in where people choose to work.
- Companies that fail to engage in meaningful social responsibility initiatives will struggle to retain top talent.

What Businesses Must Do to Prepare:

- Embed Purpose into Business Strategy – Move beyond corporate statements and take real action on climate, diversity, and ethics.

- Encourage Employee-Led Social Initiatives – Provide paid time for community service and employee-driven CSR programs.
- Create a Transparent, Values-Driven Culture – Ensure that social impact efforts align with core business operations and leadership priorities.

The next decade will bring monumental generational shifts that reshape hiring, leadership, and workplace culture. Business leaders who embrace flexibility, innovation, and employee-first policies will not only survive these changes but thrive in the new workforce landscape.

By proactively adapting to these shifts, businesses can create more engaged, purpose-driven, and future-ready workplaces.

In the next section, we will provide a self-assessment tool for business owners to measure their generational awareness and readiness for the workforce of the future.

Practical Tools: Self-Assessment for Business Owners to Measure Their Generational Awareness

Understanding and effectively managing a multigenerational workforce is no longer optional—it's a necessity for business success. With rapid shifts in workplace expectations, technological advancements, and evolving leadership dynamics, business owners must assess their generational awareness and adaptability. A lack of awareness can lead to miscommunication, disengagement, and missed opportunities, while strong generational awareness fosters innovation, inclusivity, and long-term retention.

This self-assessment tool is designed to help business owners evaluate their ability to navigate multigenerational challenges, optimize team dynamics, and create a workplace culture that meets the needs of today's workforce. By reflecting on these key areas, leaders can identify strengths, uncover gaps, and implement targeted strategies to improve engagement across generations.

1. Assessing Your Understanding of Generational Differences

How well do you understand the core values, motivations, and work styles of each generation?

- Do you recognize how Baby Boomers, Gen X, Millennials, and Gen Z differ in their approach to work, leadership, and communication?
- Can you identify what motivates employees from different generations and adjust your management style accordingly?
- Do you acknowledge generational stereotypes but avoid making blanket assumptions about employees based on their age?

Action Steps to Improve:
- Conduct workforce surveys or focus groups to understand generational preferences within your team.
- Attend leadership training or workshops on generational dynamics in the workplace.
- Encourage intergenerational mentorship programs where employees can share insights and experiences.

2. Evaluating Your Hiring and Recruitment Practices

Are you attracting talent across multiple generations?
- Do your job descriptions appeal to candidates from different generations by emphasizing skills over tenure and degrees?
- Are your hiring practices free of unintentional biases that favor or exclude specific age groups?
- Are you using modern hiring tools such as AI-driven recruitment, video interviews, and skill-based assessments to widen your talent pool?

Action Steps to Improve:
- Implement blind resume screening to minimize unconscious bias in recruitment.
- Diversify your recruitment channels by using LinkedIn, online learning platforms, and AI-driven job boards to reach a wider demographic.
- Offer internships and returnship programs to engage younger and older workers who want to transition into new roles.

3. Analyzing Your Leadership and Management Style

Do you tailor your leadership approach to accommodate different generational expectations?
- Are you using a mix of leadership styles, balancing structured guidance with flexibility?
- Do you give frequent, informal feedback to younger employees while also providing structured performance reviews for those who prefer them?
- Are you balancing workplace autonomy with clear expectations to meet the needs of both independent Gen X workers and collaborative Millennials?

Action Steps to Improve:
- Train managers to use situational leadership, adapting their approach to individual employee needs.
- Encourage multigenerational leadership teams to ensure decision-making is diverse and representative.
- Provide customized professional development plans that align with different career priorities.

4. Measuring Workplace Communication Effectiveness

Do you use communication methods that resonate with all generations?
- Are you balancing email, face-to-face meetings, instant messaging, and video calls to accommodate generational preferences?
- Do you ensure that workplace communication is clear, inclusive, and free from generational bias?
- Are employees encouraged to provide feedback on communication preferences and effectiveness?

Action Steps to Improve:
- Conduct communication audits to identify which methods work best for your workforce.
- Implement flexible communication channels that cater to different needs (e.g., Slack for quick collaboration, email for formal updates, video calls for strategic discussions).
- Train employees in effective intergenerational communication to enhance workplace relationships.

5. Reviewing Workplace Flexibility and Employee Benefits

Are your policies aligned with modern workforce expectations?
- Do you offer remote or hybrid work options for employees who prefer flexible arrangements?
- Are your benefits packages attractive across generations, addressing needs like student loan assistance, parental leave, and phased retirement options?
- Do you encourage results-based performance rather than measuring productivity based on hours worked?

Action Steps to Improve:
- Review and update workplace flexibility policies to attract and retain diverse talent.
- Offer personalized benefits that cater to different life stages (e.g., financial wellness programs for Gen Z, caregiving support for Gen X, phased retirement for Boomers).
- Foster a culture of trust and autonomy by allowing employees to manage their own schedules when possible.

6. Fostering an Inclusive and Collaborative Workplace Culture

Do you create an environment where employees across generations feel valued and included?

- Are employees encouraged to collaborate across age groups, breaking down generational silos?
- Do you promote knowledge-sharing initiatives where experienced employees can mentor younger staff and vice versa?
- Are team-building activities designed to engage a diverse workforce rather than catering to just one generation's preferences?

Action Steps to Improve:

- Implement reverse mentorship programs, where younger employees teach digital skills and older employees share leadership insights.
- Create cross-generational project teams to promote collaboration and innovation.
- Recognize contributions across all age groups through inclusive appreciation programs.

7. Assessing Adaptability to Future Generational Shifts

Are you preparing for the future of work?
- Do you stay informed about emerging workforce trends, including the expectations of Gen Alpha?
- Are you proactively adopting AI, automation, and digital transformation to remain competitive in the evolving job market?
- Do you regularly review and refine your workplace policies based on feedback from employees of all generations?

Action Steps to Improve:
- Conduct annual workforce trend analyses to anticipate generational shifts and workplace expectations.
- Pilot AI-driven training and career development tools to prepare for a tech-integrated workforce.
- Keep an open dialogue with employees about the future of work and their expectations.

This self-assessment is designed to help business owners reflect on their generational awareness and adaptability. By identifying strengths and areas for growth, leaders can implement targeted strategies to create a more inclusive, future-ready workplace.

Generational diversity is not a challenge to overcome—it's a powerful asset that, when managed effectively, drives innovation, collaboration, and long-term success. The question isn't whether the workforce will continue evolving—it's whether your business is evolving with it.

Now, as you complete this self-assessment, ask yourself: Are you leading a workplace that welcomes and maximizes the strengths of every generation? Are you building a culture that adapts to change rather than resists it? If not, now is the time to act. The future of work isn't coming—it's already here. How you choose to navigate it will define the long-term success of your organization.

I Call "BS"

Challenging the premise—because good leadership demands better questions.

Even the most well-intentioned ideas deserve scrutiny. Throughout this book, we've explored the value of generational diversity and how adapting to different work styles, motivations, and expectations can drive business success. But what about the questions that push back? What about the skepticism, the eye-rolls, and the "yeah, but..." reactions? This section is dedicated to those doubts. Because good leadership isn't about avoiding tough questions—it's about answering them.

1. Why don't we just hire all from the same generation and eliminate the friction?

Building a team from a single generation might reduce initial friction, but it also narrows the range of perspectives, skills, and problem-solving approaches. Generational diversity isn't just a challenge to manage—it's a strategic advantage. Companies that blend generations tend to be more innovative, more resilient, and better equipped to serve diverse customers.

2. Isn't all of this just overthinking? Can't we just treat everyone the same?

Fairness doesn't always mean sameness. Treating everyone exactly the same ignores the reality that people are motivated differently, communicate differently, and bring different experiences to the table. Great leaders recognize patterns and adapt their approach—not to coddle, but to connect.

3. What about industries like construction, manufacturing, or the trades—does any of this even apply there?

Yes, absolutely. While the setting might be different, people are still people. Generational differences show up in how apprentices learn, how supervisors lead, how teams collaborate, and how loyalty is built. Even in the trades, understanding what drives each generation can mean the difference between keeping talent or losing it.

4. Isn't Gen Z just entitled? Why should we adapt to them instead of them adapting to us?

Every generation is labeled negatively at some point. Boomers were once called self-absorbed, Gen X was dubbed cynical, and Millennials were mocked for being coddled. Gen Z's expectations around flexibility and mental health aren't signs of entitlement—they're signals that the workplace is changing. Adaptation isn't about catering to demands—it's about evolving to remain competitive.

5. Didn't workplaces run just fine when we all followed the same rules?

They ran fine—for the time. But what worked then may not work now. The modern workforce is more diverse, more mobile, and more values-driven. Trying to recreate the past may comfort some leaders, but it won't prepare them for the future.

6. What if generational diversity causes more harm than good?

Diversity of any kind can be challenging—but when well-managed, it leads to stronger performance. The key is intentional leadership: setting shared expectations, facilitating cross-generational dialogue, and fostering mutual respect. The friction isn't the problem. The lack of communication is.

7. Aren't younger generations too sensitive for the real world?

It's not about sensitivity—it's about emotional intelligence. Younger generations are more open about mental health, feedback, and work-life balance. That doesn't make them fragile; it makes them more self-aware. When paired with accountability, that awareness becomes a powerful asset.

8. Isn't this all just the latest HR trend?

Trends come and go—but generational dynamics have been shaping the workplace for decades. This isn't about buzzwords or bandwagons. It's about understanding the lived experiences that shape behavior and motivation. That's not a trend; that's human leadership.

9. If someone's good at their job, does their generation even matter?

Skills matter, absolutely. But generational context helps explain how those skills are applied, how feedback is received, and how someone prefers to be led or supported. You don't lead a skilled employee from Gen Z the same way you lead one from Gen X. Knowing the difference helps you get the best from both.

10. What if I don't want to change my leadership style?

That's your choice—but so is the outcome. Refusing to adapt may work in the short term, but over time, it leads to disengagement, turnover, and missed opportunities. The most successful leaders aren't the ones with the loudest voices—they're the ones who listen, learn, and evolve without losing who they are.

11. Will we ever go back to the way it was for Generation X, the Boomers, or even the Silent Generation?

Unlikely—and that's not necessarily a bad thing.

Each generation thrived in a different economic and cultural moment. The job-for-life model of the Silent Generation, the structured climb of the Boomers, and Gen X's push for autonomy were products of their time. Today's workplace is faster, more digital, and constantly evolving.

That doesn't mean we lose what worked. Values like loyalty, resilience, and work ethic can still thrive—but they need to be reimagined in modern terms. Rather than go back, we can move forward by adapting the best of the past to today's world.

12. Where does the whole idea of meritocracy come into play when managing these generations? Isn't performance what really matters most?

Merit matters—but how we define it can vary by generation.

Boomers might value visibility and hours put in. Millennials and Gen Z might focus on efficiency, innovation, or collaboration—sometimes in less visible ways. That doesn't mean one approach is better; it means performance needs to be measured more thoughtfully.

True meritocracy happens when expectations are clear, performance is judged fairly, and different strengths are valued. When done right, it creates a workplace where everyone sees a path to succeed.

In the End, Questions Make Us Better

The goal of this section isn't to shut down skepticism—it's to engage with it honestly. Every "what if," every challenge, every moment of doubt is a doorway to better leadership. When business owners take time to understand—not just react—they gain clarity, earn trust, and build workplaces that actually work. You don't need all the answers. But if you're willing to ask better questions, you're already leading differently.

So, The Future of Work is Now

The workplace isn't just changing—it has already changed. If there's one thing we've seen throughout this book, it's that each generation brings something valuable to the table. Whether it's the deep experience of Baby Boomers, the independent problem-solving of Gen X, the purpose-driven mindset of Millennials, or the digital fluency of Gen Z, we are all shaping the workforce together. The question isn't whether these generational shifts will continue—it's how we choose to respond to them.

We've explored how different generations approach work, leadership, and communication, and we've taken a deep dive into hiring, retention, and company culture in the years ahead. The reality is, no single strategy will work for every workplace. But by understanding the trends shaping the workforce and adapting accordingly, we can create environments where employees of all ages feel valued, engaged, and motivated.

A Few Things to Keep in Mind

As you reflect on what this means for your business, consider these key takeaways:

- Generational Awareness Matters – Knowing what drives each generation can help you build stronger teams, better relationships, and a more engaged workforce.

- Flexibility is Here to Stay – Employees today value autonomy, work-life balance, and purpose. Companies that embrace hybrid models, skills-based hiring, and trust-based leadership will be the ones that thrive.
- Leadership Isn't One-Size-Fits-All – Good leadership is about listening, adapting, and knowing when to offer guidance versus when to step back. Employees at different stages of their careers need different kinds of support.
- Technology Should Enhance, Not Replace, Human Connection – AI and automation are powerful tools, but they should be used to support people, not distance them from meaningful collaboration.
- A Multigenerational Workforce is an Asset, Not a Challenge – The best workplaces aren't built around one single way of thinking. When different perspectives and experiences come together, that's where the best ideas are born.

How Different Generations Approach Work, Leadership, and Engagement

To provide a clearer picture of these generational dynamics, the following insights compare work styles, leadership preferences, and engagement motivators across generations.

Work Style Comparison

Generation	Work Ethic & Attitude	Preferred Work Environment	View on Work-Life Balance
Baby Boomers (1946–1964)	Hardworking, loyal, value job security	Traditional office setting, structured roles	Work-centric, willing to put in extra hours
Gen X (1965–1980)	Independent, pragmatic, skeptical of authority	Flexible but values clear expectations	Seeks balance but prioritizes results
Millennials (1981–1996)	Purpose-driven, collaborative, tech-savvy	Hybrid or remote work, open collaboration spaces	Values work-life integration and flexibility
Gen Z (1997–2012)	Digital-first, efficiency-focused, socially conscious	Remote-first, digital workplaces, gig economy	Prioritizes mental health and work-life harmony

Leadership Preferences

Generation	Preferred Leadership Style	View on Hierarchy	Feedback Expectations
Baby Boomers	Directive, top-down leadership	Respects authority, prefers clear chains of command	Annual performance reviews, formal feedback
Gen X	Hands-off, results-driven	Values autonomy, dislikes micromanagement	Prefers constructive, direct feedback when necessary
Millennials	Collaborative, coaching-based	Prefers flat hierarchies, values inclusion	Wants continuous feedback, mentorship-based guidance
Gen Z	Transparent, adaptive	Rejects rigid hierarchies, favors decentralized decision-making	Expects instant feedback, values recognition in real-time

Engagement & Motivation

Generation	What Motivates Them	Preferred Communication Style	Retention Factors
Baby Boomers	Job stability, financial security, recognition for experience	Formal emails, in-person meetings	Competitive salaries, pension plans, prestige
Gen X	Career progression, autonomy, work-life balance	Email, direct messaging, concise communication	Career advancement, professional development, flexibility
Millennials	Purpose-driven work, social impact, growth opportunities	Instant messaging, video calls, casual communication	Meaningful work, strong company culture, leadership transparency
Gen Z	Innovation, inclusivity, fast career growth	Short-form digital communication, social media, visuals	Mental health support, diversity & inclusion, flexibility

Looking Ahead

The future of work isn't just about adapting to change—it's about understanding the people driving that change. Whether you're hiring new talent, evolving your leadership style, or rethinking workplace policies, the choices you make will shape both the experience of your employees and the long-term success of your business.

The workplaces that thrive will be those that embrace collaboration over division, adaptability over resistance, and purpose over routine. The next decade will bring both challenges and opportunities, but businesses that prioritize flexibility, communication, and generational awareness will create environments where employees of all backgrounds can do their best work.

Work has always evolved, but today, that evolution is happening faster than ever. Leaders who choose to understand and engage with generational differences—rather than dismiss them—will be the ones who succeed. Generational dynamics aren't barriers; they're opportunities to build stronger teams, foster better relationships, and drive meaningful results.

When we stop seeing generational differences as obstacles and start viewing them as strengths, we don't just create better workplaces—we build a future where every generation wins.

Afterword

You've made it through *Gen WTF*, and hopefully, you now see your workforce—and perhaps even yourself—through a new lens. Understanding generational differences isn't just an academic exercise; it's a business strategy. A workforce that understands itself is a workforce that thrives.

But knowledge without action is wasted. The real question is: what will you do with what you've learned?

You don't need to implement everything in this book at once. Instead, start small—pick just one or two insights that resonated with you and apply them. Maybe it's a shift in how you hire. Maybe it's rethinking how you communicate with employees across different generations. Maybe it's simply recognizing that what worked 10 or 20 years ago may not be the best strategy today.

This book wasn't written to convince you that one generation is better than another. It was written to give you the tools to navigate generational differences effectively. The most successful business owners and leaders don't resist change—they adapt, evolve, and lead.

The workforce will continue to change. AI will advance, workplace norms will shift, and new generations will enter the scene. But one thing will always remain true: business is about people. The better you understand them, the better your business will be.

The next step is yours to take.

Acknowledgements

Writing a book is never a solo journey, and *Gen WTF* wouldn't exist without the people who have shaped, stretched, and strengthened me along the way. This book is the result of countless conversations, experiences, and lessons learned from those who have influenced my understanding of people, leadership, and the evolving workplace.

To my family—you've been my foundation. Your support, patience, and encouragement have meant the world to me. Thank you for putting up with my late nights, endless brainstorming sessions, and the many moments where this book consumed my thoughts. I couldn't have done this without you.

To my colleagues and clients—your real-world challenges, insights, and experiences were the inspiration behind this book. Every conversation, every frustration, and every breakthrough helped shape the ideas within these pages. Thank you for trusting me, for sharing your struggles, and for allowing me to be part of your journey.

To my mentors and peers—you've challenged me, refined my thinking, and pushed me to be better. Your wisdom has helped shape not only this book but also the way I approach leadership, business, and human behavior. I'm incredibly grateful for the guidance and support you've given me over the years.

Acknowledgements

To the editors, proofreaders, and publishing professionals—your sharp eyes, thoughtful feedback, and dedication to excellence have made this book stronger. Thank you for helping me bring these ideas to life in the best way possible.

To the podcast hosts, event organizers, and thought leaders who gave me platforms to share my ideas—your spaces allowed me to test, refine, and deepen the concepts explored in this book. The discussions, debates, and shared experiences along the way have been invaluable.

To my readers—this book is for you. Whether you're a business owner, manager, leader, or just someone trying to navigate a multigenerational workplace, I appreciate you taking the time to explore these ideas with me. My hope is that *Gen WTF* serves as a guide, a resource, and maybe even a bit of a wake-up call to help you build better workplaces, stronger teams, and more meaningful connections.

And finally, to those who shaped, challenged, and strengthened me—you've taught me that understanding people is the key to success. This book is my way of passing that lesson forward.

Additional Resources

If *Gen WTF* resonated with you and you're eager to dive deeper into generational dynamics, leadership strategies, and workplace success, these handpicked resources will expand your understanding and help you put these insights into action.

Books to Help You Lead Across Generations

The Remix: How to Lead and Succeed in the Multigenerational Workplace – Lindsey Pollak
A practical guide to understanding generational differences and using them as an advantage in leadership and teamwork.

It's the Manager – Jim Clifton & Jim Harter (Gallup)
Backed by extensive workplace research, this book unpacks how managers can engage employees of all generations for maximum performance.

Drive: The Surprising Truth About What Motivates Us – Daniel H. Pink
A game-changing look at what truly drives people to succeed—beyond just salary—applicable to every generation.

Leaders Eat Last – Simon Sinek

Explores how great leaders build trust and cooperation within diverse teams, a must-read for those managing multigenerational workforces.

The Five Dysfunctions of a Team – Patrick Lencioni

A leadership fable that highlights common workplace struggles and how to foster a strong, high-performing team.

Podcasts & Online Learning for Ongoing Insights

WorkLife with Adam Grant (Podcast)

Organizational psychologist Adam Grant breaks down the science of work culture, motivation, and productivity—across all generations.

The Future of Work Podcast (Jacob Morgan)

Conversations with top business leaders about how workplaces are evolving and what that means for different generations.

Harvard Business Review (HBR) – Generational Insights Collection (Online Articles & Research)

A curated selection of research and articles on generational trends, leadership shifts, and the future of work.

Tools & Assessments to Put Learning into Practice

CliftonStrengths Assessment (Gallup) – Self-Assessment Tool
A strengths-based assessment that helps managers and employees understand how different generations bring unique value to the workplace.

LinkedIn Learning – Managing a Multigenerational Team (Online Course)
A professional development course filled with actionable strategies for leading and engaging employees of all ages.

Final Thought

The most successful workplaces don't just acknowledge generational differences—they turn them into strengths. Whether you're leading a team, hiring new talent, or just trying to work better with colleagues of different generations, these resources will help you become a more effective leader, build stronger teams, and create a workplace where every generation thrives.

About the Author

For over 30 years, Adam J. San Juan has been deeply fascinated by human behavior—what drives people, how they make decisions, and how they interact with the world around them. As a writer, speaker, and consultant, he has dedicated his career to simplifying the complexities of human dynamics and providing practical solutions for business owners, leaders, and professionals navigating an ever-evolving workforce.

His work is built on a fundamental truth: success in business and life isn't just about strategy—it's about understanding people. Through his "Human Series" of books, he has explored the three primary conflicts all people face:

- Man vs. Man — *What Are You Looking At? The Impact of Answering and How It Changes Everything* (2023)
- Man vs. Environment — *What Am I Doing Here? A Guide to the Unseen Influences of Your Surroundings* (2024)
- Man vs. Himself — *What Was I Thinking?* (forthcoming, 2025/2026)

These books have led to thought-provoking discussions on podcasts, college campuses, and corporate boardrooms, where Adam has helped individuals and organizations better understand human interaction in professional and personal settings.

His latest book, *Gen WTF*, continues this journey by tackling one of today's most pressing workplace challenges: bridging generational differences in the workforce. Drawing from firsthand experience working with business owners and multigenerational teams, Adam brings a fresh, straightforward approach to breaking down generational conflicts, hiring strategies, and leadership methods that work.

A speaker and advisor, he has helped countless professionals rethink how they hire, lead, and engage employees across different age groups. His ability to simplify the complicated and offer practical, actionable insights has made him a trusted resource for those looking to build stronger, more connected teams.

Whether you're a business owner, manager, HR professional, or simply someone who interacts with people every day, his work will challenge the way you see the world—and help you navigate it more effectively.

Made in the USA
Monee, IL
22 April 2025

4b527a70-182b-4c35-9d73-dfc208bb3341R01